EMBRACE THE SPIRIT

STEVEN HARPER

VICTOR BOOKS ®
A DIVISION OF SCRIPTURE PRESS PUBLICATIONS INC.
USA CANADA ENGLAND

Scripture quotations, unless otherwise noted, are from the *Holy Bible,
New International Version,* © 1973, 1978, 1984, International Bible Society. Used by permission of Zondervan Bible Publishers. Other quotations are from *The New King James Version,* © 1979, 1980, 1982, Thomas
Nelson, Inc., Publishers.

Recommended Dewey Decimal Classification: 248.3
Suggested Subject Heading: SPIRITUAL LIFE

Library of Congress Catalog Card Number: 87-81012
ISBN: 0-89693-311-3

VICTOR BOOKS, a division of SP Publications, Inc.
Wheaton, IL 60187

CONTENTS

ONE
The Real Thing   11

TWO
Scenes in the Drama—I   27

THREE
Scenes in the Drama—II   41

FOUR
Never Alone!   53

FIVE
A New Way to Live   66

SIX
Preparation for the Journey   78

SEVEN
We Need Each Other   90

EIGHT
Into the World   112

NINE
Streams in the Desert   125

TEN
The Edge of Adventure   143

For Further Reading   156

Notes   161

For my students and faculty colleagues
who have taught me so much
about living an authentic spiritual life,
and who have graciously received
what I have been privileged to teach them.

FOREWORD

This Spiritual Formation book is for the Christian who hears God's call to a devotional life, and wants to better serve Him in the challenges of every day. It draws on the richness of Christian spirituality through the centuries of church history, but with an application to the twentieth-century believer who is involved in society, rather than withdrawn from it.

Spiritual Formation blends the best of traditional discipleship concepts with the more reflective disciplines of an individual journey toward friendship with God. It is a lifestyle, not a program; a relationship rather than a system; a journey instead of a roadmap. It calls us into holy partnership with God for our spiritual development.

As you read this book, and then others in the series, I hope that you will receive much more than information. My prayer is that you will experience new levels of formation of your mind and heart, and find yourself drawn closer to Christ.

Steven Harper, General Editor
Associate Professor of Spiritual Formation
Asbury Theological Seminary

PREFACE

Although we have never met, I'm willing to guess that you are interested in strengthening your Christian faith and deepening your spiritual life. The great news I have for you is that God wants to come close to you, and wants to bring you close to Him. Your Christian growth is the lifelong process of closing the gap between yourself and God. In this process, you have everything to gain, and nothing to lose.

I've tried to write this book in a clear and simple style. I like to think of it as the kind of thing I'd want to say to you personally, if we could sit down and talk together about the Christian faith. At the end of each chapter, you will find a meditation page that will give you the opportunity to respond to what God is saying to you. In the footnotes, I've made numerous suggestions about how you can continue your spiritual journey after you finish the book.

But most of all, beyond the words I pray that you will hear the Word, and know that God is interacting with you. The things I have written have not left me the same, and I doubt that you will be the same after you experience them. That's the way God is—He accepts us as we are, but does not leave us as we are!

Steven Harper
Asbury Theological Seminary
Wilmore, Kentucky
1987

ONE

THE REAL THING

After a seminar I had conducted was over, Ken asked if he could drive me to the airport. I had eaten a meal in Ken's home and discovered that he was happily married, involved in the church, and reasonably fulfilled in his work. I had also noticed that he was particularly interested in the seminar on the spiritual life. As we started out for the airport, he wasted little time before he began to share deeply with me. "When I became a Christian," he said, "my life was radically changed. I was regularly and meaningfully involved in the church. But over a period of time, my enthusiasm waned, until today I am a Christian mostly by routine and habit. I have lost the joy of my faith, and sometimes wonder if I am really a Christian at all."

Years ago, I might have been shocked by such a story; but the fact is that there are a lot of people like Ken in the world who are spiritually bored. Because of their meaningful conversions and spirit-filled experiences, they can hardly believe what has happened to them. They are frightened, depressed, and sometimes even wonder how much longer they can keep going.

Ken's story is a familiar one to me because I've heard it so often, and also because I have felt the same way in the course of my own Christian walk. You too may have experienced the same frustration that Ken expressed as we drove to the airport. You cannot automatically assume that yesterday's experience will be sufficient for the future. You are ever challenged to go deeper and find resources which can strengthen and sustain you.

This book is my attempt to share with you what I have discovered about spiritual development. It includes many of the ideas and experiences which have brought reality and vitality to my faith journey and the journey of others. It is an attempt to describe reality and then to move toward it. But right here at the beginning, I must honestly tell you that I have not come to practice the kind of Christianity described here without struggle and sometimes even setbacks. I doubt that you will either. Spiritual formation is a blending of risk and reward, vulnerability and victory, and is, of necessity, intensely personal.

COMMON MISCONCEPTIONS

In coming to embrace true Christian faith, I have had to confront a number of misconceptions which I once held as true. As valuable as my faith development has been, it has not been perfect. Yours has probably not been either. So we can assume that any serious examination of faith will involve a confrontation with ideas that can mislead us.

† Perhaps the most devastating of these is the belief that right theology will promote spiritual vitality and protect us from the snares of life. The last decade in evangelical circles has witnessed an increased concern for orthodoxy. And to be sure, we had a lot of theological housecleaning to do! The sixties wallowed in heresy, even to suggesting that God was dead. But in our well-intentioned zeal to replace error with truth, we made the mistake of implying that if we could get people to believe right, they would be spiritually alive.

The last ten to fifteen years have seen a wave of teaching ministries, each designed to ensure that the truth of Christianity would be communicated with as much purity as possible. All over the country, there are believers whose notebooks and minds are filled with impressively correct information. Yet, they continue to struggle with personal problems of all kinds, and they have the gnawing suspicion that their intellectually held faith is not producing the quality of life it should, or could.

A nationally known counselor told me that the majority of his time is spent with orthodox Christians for whom the truth has become meaningless, irrelevant, or oppressive. He lamented the fact that some of his hardest cases are people whose theology is fundamentally correct.

For those of us who have equated theological truth with spiritual vitality, this first misconception is hard to even accept. Does it mean that a concern for theological truth is unimportant? By no means. But it does mean that attaining right theology will not automatically produce spiritual vitality. And this is something we are going to have to face, if we are to move to a more meaningful faith. Our correctness can lead us into what John Wesley called "dead orthodoxy." It can create a contemporary Phariseeism that causes us to lay burdens on others which we cannot bear. And perhaps worst of all, it can create an insatiable perfectionism which will have damaging negative consequences for ourselves and others.

Early in my Christian experience I ran across the book, *How Come It's Taking Me So Long to Get Better?* On the basis of the title alone, I bought it. Among other things, the author stressed that the wells of vital Christianity must go deeper than mere correctness in theology, that Christianity is a life to be lived more than it is a creed to be believed. While orthodoxy is important, we cannot allow it to become the end of our journey. Right belief alone is inadequate to produce spiritual vitality.

† Ironically, a second misconception has been that right experience will produce spiritual life. There have been a wealth of programs aimed at producing certain experiences or feelings in the believer. Proponents of this misconception have labored under the notion that if people could feel right, they would be right.

In my own tradition, to be born again or converted was

to have reached the ultimate experience with God. And so, I interpreted my conversion as being the end of a quest for God. For some of my friends, the experience was solidified all the more because they were told that what they had found could never be lost. The message was clear: we had "arrived."

Seven years later, one of my seminary professors said that no single experience would ever sustain a vital Christianity. However, in those years of intense emotion, his comments went largely unheard. The currents were flowing the other way. People were coming into the kingdom singing, shouting, and waving their hands in the air. It all looked so good, how could it possibly be inadequate?

But the passing of time has proved him right. People have come limping back to camp, testifying that their feelings gave out. Their experience ran its course. They simply could not sustain their Christianity on the basis of a single experience, no matter how right it had been. They sensed there had to be something more, even if they could not immediately describe what it was.

The problem with these first two misconceptions is not that they're wrong—they're just incomplete. No one can deny that both of them brought people into the kingdom who might not have come any other way. The problem is that they were inadequate to sustain people over a long period of time. You simply cannot build a vital and mature faith by concentrating on one element of the human personality. Christianity is comprehensive and takes the whole person into account.

† A third misconception is that spirituality is an entity in itself, somehow divorced from the rest of life. One of the earliest and most graphic examples of this perspective was seen in those few people who decided they could only be really spiritual by leaving their families. A much more common expression of this misconception was the tendency (which still persists) to turn Christianity into a privatized "me and Jesus" phenomenon

divorced from the responsibilities and routines of life.

During a time of ministry on a college campus, I was meeting with faculty members who were trying to deal with a group of students whose spirituality included a promiscuous sexuality. They seemed to see nothing inconsistent between the purity of their beliefs and the impurity of their actions. I thought back to another time of ministry in Texas when I learned that some of the leaders of a congregation were practicing blatant wife-swapping.

Such behaviors represent a new dualism on the part of professing Christians whose "spirituality" builds fences between faith and behavior. The result is an artificial spirituality which looks and sounds good, but which falls apart at the point of application. This is true not only in the area of morals, but also in the realm of ministry to the larger society. Any definition of Christianity which will allow us to hold a personal faith, but ignore its interpersonal implications, is a misconception of the highest order.

† Some Christians have bankrupted themselves by believing that true spirituality is something reserved for a select few. Before the advent of the electronic church, we could erroneously believe that the clergy were especially spiritual. And now with the influx of media ministries, it is possible to wonder if only the celebrities are truly blessed!

If we are to mature in our faith, we must see ourselves as prime candidates for a deeper walk with God. This is what Ken was searching for, as we talked in the car on the way to the airport. He suspected that there was more to Christianity than he had experienced; now he was reaching out to discover how that deeper life could be his. He was not willing to believe that only professional religious people could have it. The Spirit was moving in his life telling him that this kind of life is for every Christian.

† I've saved a fifth misconception until the last, because it

is of more recent vintage. It is also one of the more insidious cancers that eats away at the tissue of true Christianity. I'm talking about the notion that to be spiritually alive is to be materially prosperous. Nothing has done more to undercut true Christianity than this heretical notion. Teachers abound who will tell you that your faith obligates God to bless you with an increase of the things of this world. Their own lives appear to verify the principle, only because their supporters pour millions of dollars into their ministries.

Richard Foster's book, *Money, Sex, and Power,* exposes this trend to materialize the faith. In it he shows how the emphasis on money, sex, and power is actually a perversion of the three classic principles of poverty, chastity, and obedience.[1] A new generation of teachers and writers is exposing this fallacy and offering ways out of the dilemma. I hope this book will be another contribution to that end.

TRUE SPIRITUALITY

Having examined some of the misconceptions regarding the spiritual life, we are at a point where we can ask the real question, "What is true spirituality?" What is it that people have missed, even in a period of spiritual awakening? That's what I want to examine in the rest of this chapter. I believe the church has overlooked or underemphasized certain key elements in vital spirituality. The task of spiritual formation is to reintroduce these elements and help people apply them to their lives.

I want you to take Ken's place in the car so that we can visit about ways and means of regaining the note of joy in our Christianity. I think I've told you enough already for you to know I'm not looking for a shallow or counterfeit joy. Rather, I am out to find the kind of life Jesus described in the word *blessed.* Surely His was no shallow piety! And the clear indication from Scripture is that ours does not have to be either. So, let's use our time to find out something about an approach to faith that can keep us going for a lifetime.

† First of all, we begin with a recognition of key elements, and the primary one is that you and I are made in the image of God. That's certainly not a new idea, but it may be a new realization, especially as a foundation block for spiritual life. Yet, at the apex of creation, when God desired to create human life, it was His choice that such life be made in His image (Genesis 1:26).

Teaching about the image of God has traditionally emphasized rationality (mind), affection (emotion), volition (will), and eternity (life) with God. This definition needs one more dimension. To be made in the image of God also means that we are created for relationship. Our being made *like* God was so that we could have fellowship *with* God.

We cannot relate fully with things unlike ourselves. I have a wonderful cocker spaniel named Heath. He is able to understand certain basic words and commands, but we will never be able to sit down and have a full-fledged conversation. Heath is not a human and I am not a dog. And because we are not alike, we cannot fully relate.

For reasons not completely known to us, God wanted to relate in a special way to the human part of the creation. But for that to happen, we had to be "like God." Our being made in the image of God is the most important thing that can ever be said of us, because it means that in our essence, we are made for a relationship with the Divine!

Several times in Scripture God says, "Be holy, for I am holy."[2] Is this a command without hope of fulfillment? I don't think so. Rather, I believe it is more of an invitation. It is God saying to humanity, "Share My life in ways that are truly amazing!" The reason it can be a gracious invitation is that we already share in the essence of God through our creation.

Writers on the spiritual life in times past have often

spoken about "the life of God in the soul of man." This is possible because we are made in God's image. Through our creation in the image of God, we can experience the initial and continuing expressions of spiritual life.

† Related to this is a second key element: the Incarnation continues through incarnation. You may have to read that a few times to get the gist of it. It's another way of saying what Martin Luther said, that Christians are "little Christs." We're not talking here about a messianic complex. That's a medical problem we handle through institutionalization. But we shouldn't let the neurotic expressions derail us from the real thing. While we never become Christ (messianic complex), we can become "like Christ." In fact, I believe this is the most important teaching in the New Testament outside of the call to conversion.

Jesus spoke about it when He said, "Abide in Me" (John 15:4-7). Paul's favorite expressions were "Christ in you" and "you in Christ." In fact, he said that the secret of Christianity is "Christ in you, the hope of glory" (Colossians 1:27). What does all this mean? Simply that Jesus Christ came into the world, not only to die for us—but to live through us. Just as creation makes us "like God," so re-creation or new birth makes us "like Christ."

This is vitally important. The call to be like God, while marvelous, is more philosophical than personal. But the call to be like Christ is intensely personal. As E. Stanley Jones used to say, "Christianity is not Word remaining Word—no, it is Word becoming flesh." In like manner, our spirituality is personal. It is becoming "like Christ," as Christ Himself comes to live in us and through us.

When I first read passages like those quoted above, I honestly believed Jesus and Paul were talking about something symbolic. I felt they were straining under the limitations of human language to describe a divine reality. However, I now believe both Jesus and Paul were describing an actual reality! And that's why "Christ in you" is the hope of glory. Jesus actually offers Himself to us, and through that offer enters our lives to make us more like Him!

I began to realize this reality after I was married. Even as newlyweds, we would catch ourselves saying, "I knew you were going to say that." We came to a place in our relationship where we could anticipate the other with an amazing degree of accuracy. As the years passed, we found ourselves saying, "I knew that's what you were thinking."

Did this ability come through some mystical, extrasensory power? No! It came through living together every day for years and years. It came through observing each other in a wide variety of circumstances. It came through long conversations in which we shared our hearts with each other. And after such prolonged intimacy, we have something of a "common mind."

I believe this is exactly what the Bible means when it calls us to have "the mind of Christ" (Philippians 2:5). It is not calling for some symbolic experience. No, it is asking us to live close to Christ, and to allow Him to live close to us—for so long that we begin to see life as He would see it, respond to it as He would respond, and act in it as He would act. That's not symbolic!

William Barclay said that Jesus puts a face on God. And it's a vitally necessary face if we are to live a truly spiritual life, for in Christ, the abstract is made concrete. The philosophical is made personal. The possible becomes actual. We see what it means to be made in the image of God, now fleshed out in a human being to the fullest extent. We have a model, not just a message. We have an example, not just a command.

Unfortunately, some promoters of the New Age Movement have perverted this idea of becoming like Christ to mean that we are all God. This is not what I'm talking about. The Bible teaches that we are human beings who have been made alive with the life of Christ through the Spirit. Our life is becoming increasingly saturated with the life of Christ. We can say what

Paul said, "For me to live is Christ" (Philippians 1:21). This is what it means for the Incarnation to continue in and through us.

† This leads us to a third key element which flows out of the first two. Life is sacred in its essence. Created to be "like God" and redeemed to be "like Christ," we can no longer relate to any other person from a purely secular point of view. Everyone we meet is, by creation, just a little lower than the angels. And if they are Christians, they and we share a common redemption through Christ and life "in Christ."

If we understand the sacredness of life, we can never again manipulate others to our advantage. We cannot remain silent or inactive when the forces of dehumanization work anywhere in the world. We can never lump human beings into a group and call them "the enemy."

The essence of Christianity is transformation. God has come to us in Christ to redeem us from sin and to so work in us that we are changed increasingly into the likeness of Christ. We begin to see life with a new set of eyes and hear it with a new set of ears. We live out our days on earth with a new set of values and motivations. We realize that true spirituality includes the key elements which we have been discussing, and we take action to consciously apply their reality to our lives.

FRIENDSHIP WITH GOD

As we incorporate the key elements mentioned above into our lives, we recognize the relational nature of the faith. But how we interpret that relationship varies. Some tend toward a laissez-faire attitude which would have God saying, "You are Mine. Enjoy yourself and don't worry too much about how you live." Others tend toward a legalistic understanding which would have God saying, "You are Mine, but if you want to stay Mine, you'll have to be sure and play by the rules—all of them." And in between is a variety of approaches.

How shall we define the relationship Jesus came to offer? After nearly a quarter of a century in the Christian faith, and after exploring a number of possibilities, I am convinced that the primary relationship can be described in the word *friendship*. Jesus came to offer us friendship with God. He said, "No longer do I call you servants, for a servant does not know what his master is doing; but I have called you friends, for all that I heard from My Father I have made known to you" (John 15:15, NKJV).

For three years the disciples had walked in what might be called "uninformed obedience." They had occasional glimpses of insight and understanding; but for the most part, they were continuing to have trouble figuring out who Jesus was and what He was doing. Like slaves, they were on the outside looking in on events that were beyond their ability to comprehend. That had to change if they were to perpetuate the faith after Christ was gone. Mere servanthood was not enough.

It still isn't. As long as you base your relationship with Christ on duty, obligation, and habit, you are skating on the edge of destruction. As long as you view yourself as an outside spectator, you run the risk of not having enough when the going gets rough. Unless you are "in Christ" and Christ is "in you," you run the risk of trading in the real thing for a lifetime of inadequate substitutes. Jesus knew that about His own original disciples, and He knows it about us.

Friendship with God is what we're after. It's the only kind of relationship that will take us where we want to go. It's the only kind of relationship that will hold us up when the pressure weighs us down. It's the only kind of relationship that will make Christianity our life rather than our duty. The saints of the centuries have known this, but contemporary Christianity has fallen prey to a dangerous case of spiritual amnesia.

True spirituality is not just another version of "easy believism." It is not another "program" that you can master in ten lessons—or ten years, not another self-mastery technique. It is not just trying harder and doing better. No, true spirituality is a matter of pure grace coupled with all the commitment you can give in return.

Henri Nouwen has described the spiritual life as a movement from inauthenticity to authenticity.[3] I want to use the idea of "movement" to give some specificity to what we're talking about in this idea of friendship with God. As we've seen, the movement is from servant to friend. Within this are some other movements which clarify what this means.

† First of all, it is a movement from legalism to grace. Martin Luther said that the greatest day in the life of a Christian is when he moves from hearing God say, "You must!" to hearing Him say, "You may." This means that the whole basis of faith shifts from threat to privilege. God ceases to be the cosmic policeman and becomes the loving guide.

It is amazing—and tragic—how many Christians are running scared in their relationship with God. After I talked about this in one of my classes, a student stopped by my office to say that the hour had been a genuine God-moment in his life. For the first time in his life he had seen a God of love, rather than one of demanding legalism. He left rejoicing!

Does your God demand or invite? If yours demands, you have yet to meet the Father of Jesus. The God and Father of our Lord Jesus Christ invites. This is not a mushy invitation without consequences if we refuse to accept. It is not emotional sentimentalism. Rather, it is an invitation to become part of a lifestyle that is only possible by grace. And it's an invitation that more nearly saddens God than angers Him when it's rejected. If those who walk away from God would look over their shoulders, they would see tears in His eyes—not a club in His hands.

In our society, it is hard to grasp the idea that the spiritual life is lived by grace. We so often live under the banner of "You get what you pay for," and we tend to include Christianity in this as well. It is virtually inconceivable to us that authentic spirituality comes by grace, and not by keeping some predetermined set of rules. But God comes with an offer that only He can supply. We cannot earn it or merit it. Real spirituality requires a movement from legalism to grace.

† Second, it is a movement from the periphery to the center. Slaves are on the outside. They don't really feel a part of the family. They merely receive orders and then dutifully carry them out. But friends are on the inside. They have a sense of what is going on. In fact, they sometimes help to shape what is happening. This is the kind of life Jesus offers to us.

Again, this is a hard concept to grasp, for even in our church life, we often feel like outsiders. Plans and programs are established without our input, and we are told to contribute. Worship services are scheduled and we are told to attend. In a subtle way, this can create the idea that God considers us outsiders.

But the "grace life" is not one of merely receiving orders and carrying them out. It is not one of passive obedience, but of active involvement. It means being part of the family, one whose feelings and opinions are respected. While we will never fully understand God, we are invited to understand many of His ways. Through prayer and reflection we are invited to interact with His will. True spirituality instills within us the realization that we are not simply spectating, but rather participating.

I can still remember the time when one of my lay leaders in a church I was pastoring came alive to this truth. For years, he had been a duty-oriented church member. He believed in the church and supported it with his prayers, presence, gifts, and service. But when it came to attitude, he felt like an outsider. He left the running of things largely up to God and the pastor. His job, he reasoned, was to wait for the "word" and then support it.

However, a series of events brought him to the place of realizing that he had been invited by Christ to have a hand in shaping the direction of the church. His call came with respect to missions. He became actively involved in a national mission-sending agency, and even went on some mission trips himself—using his agricultural and mechanical skills. The change in him, from looking in on the work of the church to being part of the family, was revolutionary.

We move into vital Christianity as we begin to see ourselves as twentieth-century disciples—just as involved in the work of the kingdom as the first-century disciples. It means that our lives become channels through which the Holy Spirit can move. Our talents become tools in His hands to do things that might not otherwise be done.

† Related to this is the third movement, from job to vocation. We often tend to view Christianity as our Sunday job rather than as our vocation. Someone has said that it is too easy to let Christianity be a part of life, rather than life itself.

In talking one time with a minister from a Communist country, I mentioned that it seemed inconsistent for an atheistic society to allow churches to exist. He responded by saying, "Christianity is no threat as long as you can contain it to one day a week. It is only when it becomes a way of life that the authorities seek to stamp it out."

I believe many people in our secularized society would say the same thing. Christianity is no threat as long as it is a one-day-a-week thing. A pagan culture will tolerate Christian values as long as they don't infringe upon the values of the marketplace. Time and time again laypeople have said to me, "The most difficult part of being a Christian is living it where I work."

Unfortunately, many professing Christians have defined their faith in terms of tight compartments—a certain day of the week, certain moments in the day, and with certain relationships. That keeps it safe and manageable, and innocuous. If we are to live a life of true spirituality, we must learn that Christianity is our vocation. It is not something we do now and then. It is who we are all the time.

I asked a friend who works in a bank how often he sees counterfeit money. "Almost every day," he replied. I asked him how he could spot the phony stuff when it passed through his hands, what indicators he had been taught to look for. His answer surprised me. He said, "There are many varieties of counterfeit currency. We learn to spot the fake money by recognizing and handling the real thing. Once you know the real thing, you can spot the counterfeit."

Spiritual life is the same way. There are many variations that profess to be the real thing, but which are actually counterfeits. It is not our task to go around pointing out every aberration we see. Rather, it is our calling to come in touch with the real thing. The authentic becomes its own validator, and the indicator of what is false.

That's why Jesus made it a point to tell His disciples that the real thing is friendship. He offers Himself to us as our Friend, and He asks us to be His friends in a relationship which is unparalleled. In the remaining chapters of this book, we will examine some of the dimensions of that relationship.

SEEKING AUTHENTICITY

From that time on, Jesus began to preach, "Repent, for the kingdom of heaven is near."

Matthew 4:17

PRACTICE SILENCE

Sit quietly until the noise of your own thoughts subsides. Imagine Jesus coming to you to help you make the journey toward authentic spirituality.

PRACTICE REFLECTION

Repentance means to change your mind. Consider any places in your own life where repentance is in order.

Friendship with Jesus is the goal of authentic spiritual life. Consider how coming to know Jesus as *your* Friend will facilitate your journey toward authenticity.

PRACTICE RESOLUTION

List two or three attitude or behavior changes you want to make, to move from inadequate faith toward authentic faith.

PRACTICE PRAYER

Ask Jesus to come into your life with grace to enable you to make good on your resolutions. Thank Him for the gift of His friendship to you.

PRACTICE READING

Psalm 27:7-10 and Matthew 28:20

T W O

SCENES IN THE DRAMA—I

The spiritual life is alive. It moves. It pulsates with the life of God. I'm sure that's the reason I like to speak of the spiritual life as a drama. In a theatrical presentation there are numerous scenes, but continuous story line and character development. As the play develops, we often say, "The plot thickens." So also in spiritual formation, there is progress and development without leaving anything behind. In this chapter we want to examine some of the major scenes in our spiritual formation.

DEFINITION

A play must have a story line, a plot. Without that, there would be no movement and meaning to the drama. One scene would not connect with another. All would be chaos. So too in the the spiritual life we must have some understanding of what we are about, or we risk going off in all directions, wasting precious time and energy, and perhaps even ending up at the wrong place.

I like the story of the traveling salesman who was driving down a rural backroad when he came upon a surprising sight. On the side of a large barn was a row of archery targets. The amazing thing was that in the center of each bull's-eye was an arrow. The salesman was so taken by the accuracy of the shots that he pulled to the side of the road to inquire who the expert marksman was.

27

He found the farmer and asked who had shot the arrows into the barn. The farmer said, "I did." Taken aback, the salesman exclaimed, "You mean that you can shoot an arrow into the bull's-eye every time? That's incredible!" The farmer looked down at his feet and mumbled, "Shucks, ain't nothin to it. I just shoot the arrow into the barn and then paint the target around it."

This illustrates why definition is so important. Without it we can shoot off in all directions, and then try to legitimize our efforts by painting false targets around our spiritual arrows. In chapter 1, we established our fundamental definition of true spirituality: friendship with God. This definition is not only confirmed in Scripture, but has been developed in the centuries of Christian history.

We must grasp this definition firmly, because most of us have lived in America where a membership mentality pervades our thinking. We belong to a myriad of clubs and organizations. We know what it is like to be a member, even of the church. But from a spiritual formation standpoint, we cannot accept a membership mentality as our working definition of Christianity. It will not produce the quality and vitality of spiritual life which we are seeking.

If the idea of friendship with God is very new, you may want to reread chapter 1 and reflect on what it means for you.

DESIRE

Once you have grasped what you're after, you must ask, "How much do I want this in my life?" This is a critical question. You've lived long enough to know you can understand something without wanting it. And if you've been too attached to a membership mentality, you also know that you can keep on being active members without adopting this new definition of Christianity. On the surface, you may sense interest in this kind of spiritual life, but on further examination, may need to take a deeper look.

I compare this scene with the fork in the road which Jesus eventually reached with His disciples. You can see it happening in John 6:25-69, where Jesus began to shift the emphasis from miraculous signs and wonders to identifying directly with Him. The crowds realized this was a "hard saying." It's one thing to be committed to someone who can provide a few blessings now and then. It's another thing to commit your life to one who calls for the most intensive of relationships. So John records, "From this time many of His disciples turned back and no longer followed Him" (John 6:66). Jesus had to test the hearts of the disciples to see if their desire was to follow Him in this more radical way.

Long ago, the Prophet Jeremiah spoke for God when he said, "You will seek Me and find Me when you seek Me with all your heart" (29:13). This is the issue of desire, and it confronts us daily in the drama of spiritual formation. It leads to the prayer of the psalmist, "Search me, O God, and know my heart; test me and know my anxious thoughts. See if there is any offensive way in me, and lead me in the way everlasting" (139:23).

Definition flows into desire—we experience that in our human loves. I still remember the first time I saw Jeannie. As we came to know each other better, my understanding of her came increasingly to fit the definition of the kind of woman I wanted for my wife. At some point, however, I had to move beyond definition to desire, and come to the place where I *wanted* her to be my wife—so much so that I was willing to ask her. Yes, there was a temptation to cold feet and turning back from what I knew. And yes, there was a period of soul-searching. But my heart's desire was for Jeannie, and that desire led me to action.

We must never underestimate the power and necessity of our will in spiritual formation. Although the grace of God can overwhelm us, it never forces us to do anything we are not willing to do. A mark of cultic and pagan religions is the uncontrollable urge which causes people to say and do things they never intended. A mark of true Christianity is a blending of God's grace and our willingness to allow that grace to work in and through us. If God is giving you a hunger and a thirst for a deeper spiritual life, then you are into the scene of desire.

DISCERNMENT

Discernment, as I have used it here, is not a gift of the Spirit, or a mystical experience. It is an understanding of what spirituality is. This discernment is necessary because without it we may view spiritual formation as another "self-help program" to come down the pike, or another fad in the church. If we take up either viewpoint, we will miss the spiritual life God has for us.

† There are two problems in these misconceptions. For one thing, the focus in spiritual formation is not on the self but on Christ who transforms the self. The problem with so many self-help programs is that they focus on the self. Tapes, techniques, and seminars all become tools to help us be better, do better, function better. If we focus on the self in spiritual formation, we will miss true spirituality. It is imperative that we distinguish between "selfishness" and "spiritual development." The differences are often subtle, but very significant.

Selfishness says, "God exists to serve me. Religion is a means of self-improvement. It makes me feel better, live better, etc. It exists for me." True spirituality recognizes that as humans we are meant to grow, develop, and mature. God has made us with this kind of dynamism. But our growth and development is not an "end," but rather a "means" to a greater end—life with God and service for Him. This is why we must frequently ask ourselves if our Christianity is self-centered or Christ-centered. The answer we come up with makes all the difference.

† Secondly, discernment is necessary because spiritual formation is not a program. We have been conditioned to think programatically when it comes to our faith. Nearly everything we

experience in Christianity has a beginning point and an ending point. Denominations adopt annual emphases. Churches have special concerns. Programs come and go. Even a book like this can cause you to think that spiritual formation is a program, if you're not careful.

It is vital to discern the difference between spiritual formation as a program, and spiritual formation which makes use of effective programs. Anything which enables us to grow in the grace and knowledge of Jesus Christ is to be used and celebrated. But we must not view any program as offering the last ounce of spirituality. No book, tape, or seminar can do that.

This is one reason why our Roman Catholic friends look with wonder at us Protestants. Spiritual formation has been in their bloodstream for two thousand years. It has never been programmed or contained in any single resource, century, or movement. Rather, it has been seen as a life lived until death—a life which seeks to be increasingly conformed to Christ. It is a way of life in the world lived by the grace of God through the power of the Holy Spirit.

Even our educational system can mislead us about spiritual formation, if we think of life as a series of graduations. A much more accurate understanding of education is as an experience which *prepares* us for something. Education is not the end, but rather the means to a greater end. In like manner, spiritual formation is a lifelong series of preparations. We need to pray for the vision which will not allow any termination point or retirement age to creep into our spirituality.

I'm thankful that God has put some people in my life who have been examples in this regard. Although I only met him once, E. Stanley Jones has served to remind me of the lifelong dimension of Christianity. As I read his writings, I encounter one who never stopped living. To the end of his life, new ideas and discoveries kept attaching themselves to the main ingredients in his faith. Even after he suffered a major stroke, he wrote a final book in which he said that his faith continued to be alive and important.[1]

Closer to home, Dr. J.C. McPheeters was God's reminder to me of the unending development of the Christian faith. I met Dr. McPheeters long after he had retired as president of Asbury Theological Seminary. But in reality, Dr. Mac never retired—he didn't know the meaning of the word! I still vividly recall his last chapel sermon at the seminary when he took the occasion to tell the students what "new thing" God was doing in his life. He never stopped maturing in his faith.

Do you have any examples like this in your experience? I hope so. It is absolutely essential in spiritual formation to understand that Christianity has no end. If we are being formed by the Spirit, then the last day we live on this earth will be a day of development. God's grace is sufficient to keep us growing all our days.

DESIGN

If we recognize this ongoing aspect of spiritual formation, we are ready to move to the next scene in the drama, that of design. It is here that spiritual formation becomes exciting and challenging, as we tailor our spiritual development to the unique, unrepeatable people we are. For we discover that God has a plan of formation in mind for us that is as special as we are.

One of my favorite definitions of spiritual formation is "designing your own game with God."[2] I like this because it sounds the note of individuality. It is a reminder that God does not want to give us a form of spiritual life identical to any other Christian.

This is so important, because we are often tempted to copy the spirituality of someone else. This is natural, especially if the other person is one of our spiritual heroes or has had a special influence in our life. But if we move in the direction of copying, we will soon be off course.

Do you remember the story of David and Goliath? When David presented himself to Saul as one who would fight the giant, the king's first move was to dress David in his own armor. Because David was not used to such battle gear, he rattled and clanked around until he said, "I cannot go in these, because I am not used to them." In effect, David was saying, "I have to fight the giant in my own way."

But his way was unusual. He took five smooth stones and a slingshot and moved forward to fight Goliath. At this point in the story, I can almost hear the Israelite army saying, "No way. He's done for! Everyone knows you don't fight giants like that." Even Goliath made fun of the boy. But the next thing we hear is the sound of a giant falling to the ground. David killed the giant—in his own way.

I can remember times as a young pastor when people would come to me saying, "Steve, can you help me with my spiritual life?" And I also remember jumping to the conclusion that what had worked for me would no doubt work for them. So I would usually recommend a book or a pattern of devotion that I had found beneficial. A few weeks would go by, and they would be in my office again. And they would still be asking, "Can you help me with my spiritual life?"

I was confused. I had responded sincerely, giving them the best I had to offer. I had sent them off with proven techniques and materials, and I couldn't understand why they came back unfulfilled. Gradually, it dawned on me that I had omitted the most important part—I had failed to recognize their uniqueness. I had handed them materials without first finding out about them.

God's design for us begins by taking our uniqueness into account. People come before plans. And when I began to see things that way, I discovered some important elements in the design.

† The most important element is the person, made in the image of God. That gives each of us inestimable value. Now we need to add to that the fact that no two of us express that image in the same way. Genetics, environment, psychology, etc. combine to produce the one-of-a-kind person each of us is. Therefore, it stands to reason that if God takes the trouble to make us each different, we should anticipate difference and uniqueness in our spiritual lives as well.

Look at your fingers. At first glance they look similar. But look again. Look closely. Then you discover that the fingerprints on your fingers are totally different. No two are alike. And even more astounding, no other human being has any fingerprint like yours! You are unique. Your fingerprints are a physical reminder of the uniqueness of your spirit.

Those who study personality development remind us of how different elements in one's personality combine and interact to produce a special individual. [3] The more I study their findings, the more insight I find regarding the spiritual life. And when I recall that Paul said, "Christ in *you*, the hope of glory," I realize that he had in mind a different "you" for each person to whom he wrote. It is when we combine Christ-centeredness with human uniqueness that we are ready to see a beautiful design unfold.

We can begin to get in touch with our personality through the use of certain evaluative instruments. [4] The test results show us our basic preferences, the elements of personality that we tend to use most of the time. As we become aware of our basic personality type, we can see how the use of it can facilitate spiritual growth. For example, an introvert can more easily practice silence and meditation than can an extrovert. A thinking person will be moved more by the power of an idea, while a feeling person will find motivation in the emotions. And these are but two of hundreds of insights which can come from looking at personality theory.

A word of clarification is in order, since I find that some

Christians are hesitant to use such testing instruments in relation to spiritual growth. This fear is unfounded so long as we remember that the results are not co-equal with divine revelation. Psychological inventories are not the sixty-seventh book of the Bible. They are merely windows through which we can gain insight into ourselves. To treat them as the final word is to exaggerate their usefulness.

Getting in touch with personality is a way of reminding ourselves that there is a relationship between spirituality and personality. It assures us that God has chosen to work through us, not around us. This in itself is a revelation for those who have believed that God didn't really like them all that much. And you know the rest—people who do not believe God loves them as they are will construct artificial personalities which they feel are more acceptable.

I had an experience early in my Christian walk that informs my faith even today. It happened as I was walking down the street in Seymour, Texas. As I passed the Post Office, I noticed the Army recruiting poster with Uncle Sam pointing his bony finger at me and saying, "I want you." God used that poster to say to me, "Steve, that's what I want—I want *you.*" You see, at that time I was patterning much of my Christianity after Peter Marshall and Billy Graham. It was as if God said, "I already have a Peter Marshall and a Billy Graham. What I'm looking for is a Steve Harper. I want you."

This does not mean that we stop learning from others or that we should not use anything from their lives for our enrichment. But it does mean that we will not sell our individuality for anyone else's pattern. Instead, recognizing and celebrating that our personality is itself a beautiful gift from God, we will seek to fully incorporate it into our spiritual formation.

† A second element in the design lies in the gifts of the Spirit. Here too we are fortunate to have resources to help us discover and exercise our gifts.[5] If our personality tells us about

our created uniqueness, then the gifts of the Spirit we receive tell us about our re-created uniqueness. If personality is what I am naturally, the gifts are what I am supernaturally.

We each find that we are given certain gifts; we do not receive them all. While selectivity reminds us of our uniqueness, it also creates a sense of dependency. It causes us to see the necessity of living our faith in community, in the church. The design of the gifts of the Spirit is one of the best guards against a privatized, isolated spirituality, for to consider our gifts is to also consider our relation to other Christians.

The gifts of the Spirit give us clues as to how we best function for the good of the kingdom. In this regard, I'm frequently asked if I think the lists of the gifts of the Spirit[6] are exhaustive or representative. Personally, I think they are exhaustive. I base this on Paul's comment in 1 Corinthians 12:4-6, "There are different kinds of gifts, but the same Spirit. There are different kinds of service, but the same Lord. There are different kinds of working [results], but the same God who works all of them in all men."

The key lies in the words *gifts, service,* and *workings* (results). When seen in this light, the gifts become much more pervasive than they might first seem. For example, if your gift is teaching, it can be exercised through different services: teaching a Sunday School class, teaching from the pulpit, teaching a short-term course, etc. Furthermore, the gift of teaching can have a variety of results: instruction, conversion, edification, comfort, strengthening, etc. By so expanding all the gifts, you can see how many expressions there can be.

I know a woman who has the gift of helps. That one gift expresses itself through a number of channels: supporting the larger ministry of the church, filling in as needed on certain projects, undergirding people during times of crisis and need, etc. Her spiritual formation flows along these kinds of lines. Her supernatural gift, working in combination with her personality, results in a ministry that is unique to her and effective in the church. It can be the same for each of us.

Through discovering and using the gifts of the Spirit, we find our niche in God's larger plan. As we exercise them, we experience great joy and fulfillment, as the Holy Spirit works through us to accomplish that which is well pleasing in His sight. The linking together of personality traits with spiritual gifts helps us to see the truth of the psalmist's words, "I am fearfully and wonderfully made" (139:14).

† A third aspect of the design is the fruit of the Spirit (Galatians 5:22-23). If the gifts of the Spirit describe what we do—conduct, the fruit describes who we are—character. The gifts relate to our doing, the fruit to our being. Spiritual formation emphasizes the cultivation of the fruit of the Spirit, because in so doing we increase the characteristics of Christ in our lives. He is the perfect revelation of the fruit, and through the Holy Spirit, those same qualities are manifested in and through us.

It's important to remember that the fruit of the Spirit is singular. There are not nine fruits. Rather, there is one fruit which contains nine aspects. This means that we cannot choose some of the fruit to the exclusion of the rest. We cannot say, for example, "Well, I'll take some joy, but I don't want anything to do with kindness." No, they come together, and all of them are to be consciously cultivated in our lives. Just as we do not grow equally in all aspects of our maturing, so the fruit of the Spirit does not grow equally, but we will not be content to let any wither.

It is in the fruit of the Spirit that we evaluate our maturity. The Christians at Corinth had all the gifts, but they were seriously lacking in the fruit. That's why Paul had to put the great love chapter right in the middle of his discussions about gifts. Spiritual formation likewise puts the fruit of the Spirit right in the middle of Christian growth. True spirituality is rooted in character, and nothing less than the life of Christ can suffice.

Furthermore, it is clear that the fruit of the Spirit is character in action. Each element of the fruit can and must be exemplified in daily living. Love, joy, peace, patience, kindness, goodness, faithfulness, gentleness, and self-control make no sense except as they find expression in life. The fruit of the Spirit becomes the focus of true spirituality because in this our attitudes and actions are wedded.

Here is where attention to the devotional classics can be so helpful in our growth. The writers had a term for focusing on the fruit of the Spirit. They called it "practicing the virtues." The virtues were the biblical fruit expressed in everyday living. Entire manuals of devotion were developed to help people put the fruit into practice. Our predecessors in the faith knew better than we that you cannot speak of spiritual formation apart from a serious study and application of the fruit of the Spirit.

† A fourth element in the design is the disciplines of the spiritual life. There are practical resources and actions to help Christians get in touch with the disciplines and put them into practice.[7] John Wesley referred to the disciplines as "the means of grace." By that he meant the disciplines are the channels through which God usually conveys grace to and through His people.

I like the way Richard Foster categorizes the disciplines. He says there are inward disciplines, outward disciplines, and corporate disciplines.[8] He recognizes that Christians will use these in different ways, as situations in life call for one more than the others. The function of the spiritual disciplines is to enable us to do what needs to be done.

This aspect of spiritual formation is so important that I want to consider the disciplines in more detail in chapter 6. For now it is sufficient to see them as integral to our overall design in spiritual formation. The disciplines are the tools God gives us to put our spirituality into practice. When they are seen and used in this way, the disciplines will never be viewed or practiced selfishly.

When you attend a drama, there is usually an intermission roughly halfway through. It gives you a chance to take a break, stretch your legs, and think about what you've seen and heard so far. I think now is a good time for an intermission in our spiritual formation drama. We have already looked at definition, desire, discernment, and design. In the next chapter we will continue the drama, to show how we can apply these to our lives.

BECOMING PART OF THE CAST

Come, follow Me, and I will make you fishers of men.   Mark 1:17

PRACTICE SILENCE

Think of Jesus as the divine Director of your drama. Imagine yourself on the stage, fully attentive to the guidance of the Master.

PRACTICE REFLECTION

What are one or two dreams and desires which you would be thrilled to see Jesus fulfill in and through you?

What are two or three personality traits which you believe are strengths in your formation?

PRACTICE RESOLUTION

Allow Jesus to have full access into your life, recognizing that He will develop you lovingly.

PRACTICE PRAYER

Take your dreams and personality traits and pray the following prayer, including them one at a time: "Lord, I present my _____, as a living sacrifice, holy and acceptable to You."

PRACTICE READING

Psalm 23:1-3 and 2 Peter 3:18

THREE

SCENES IN THE DRAMA—II

Sit back and relax. The intermission is over, and the curtain is rising on the second half of our drama. In the first half we saw some of the basic elements of the spiritual life. Now the drama moves toward its conclusion, with scenes that will help us and enrich our friendship with God.

DISCIPLINE

A personal design in the spiritual life will mean very little if we lack the discipline to make it work. Through discipline, we bring our uniqueness into harmony and focus. Discipline is the dynamic which holds and transmits into real life the basic elements of spiritual formation.

If there is anything people aren't interested in today, it's discipline. Ours is the "hang loose" generation. We have fast cars, fast food, and we'd like fast spirituality as well. We thrive on the instant but have trouble with the long-term. Discipline conjures up a host of negative images. We think of a God who takes us out to the woodshed for a good thrashing. Discipline sounds like hard work; we much prefer the quick fix and the shortcut.

It is hard for many people to even understand what Richard Foster means when he calls discipline the "doorway to liberty."[1] But that's precisely what it is; and if we are to mature in the spiritual life, we must come to see discipline this way.

Otherwise, we will continue to view it negatively, as a constrictive aspect of life.

Perhaps an illustration will show us how discipline is liberating. Sometimes I long to be able to sit down at a piano and play a piece of music. When I was five years old, I took piano lessons and did remarkably well for one so young. But I lacked discipline to keep going, and my parents did not insist. So I quit. Today, it is as though I never took a single lesson. I am not free to play the piano.

Only disciplined people can do what needs to be done when it needs to be done. The rest may wish they could, but they will find themselves unable to rise to the occasion. Discipline takes us where we want to go. To be sure, it is not automatic or painless, but it is the means to a deeper, desired end.

Discipline is an attitude rather than an action. We've seen the usefulness of *disciplines* in the first part of our drama. But *discipline*—attitude—is deeper than *disciplines*—actions. The disciplines become meaningful and useful to us only because they flow out of an inner commitment to be a person of discipline.

Several years ago I was invited to conduct a School of Prayer in an Annual Conference of the United Methodist Church. I was the fifth speaker in what had become an annual event, and the invitation I received was specific: "This will be our fifth year for the School of Prayer. In each of the previous four we have learned about one of the spiritual disciplines. However, our participants are reporting that knowing the disciplines is not enough. They need help in finding the motivation to put into practice what they know. We want you to speak to us on the subject of discipline."

I don't usually get very far in a seminar on this subject without someone asking, "Is it possible to conjure up discipline?" Or sometimes a person will put it this way, "How do you go about acquiring an attitude of discipline?" Both questions are really asking the same thing. In order for me to answer, I have to speak about what I have done, and still do, in order to be a disciplined person.

For me, it has often been a matter of going back to the element of desire and really living with it for a while. My track record reveals that I lose my sense of discipline when I allow too much distance between me and my desire. When I start living my Christianity by habit rather than by desire, it isn't long before discipline starts to suffer. So I try to include regular periods of time when I intentionally focus on my desire. I go back to what makes Christianity "come alive" for me, and I drink from the waters of that desire.

My good friend Ken Kinghorn says we should all go back frequently and reflect on the hour we first believed. Can you do that? Can you go back to that place where God became more than just a word to you? That experience in which you consciously chose Jesus Christ to be Lord of your life, over all the other alternatives? Returning to such places can relight the fires of desire. I find when I do that, it is not long before my willpower makes a new resolution that heads me back in the direction of discipline.

Related to that, but beyond it, is the fact that I frequently have to keep a sense of discipline in my life simply by staying at it. The alarm goes off, and I get up—no matter what. The time for prayer is at hand, and I pray. The book is there to be read, and I read it. The serving deed waits to be done, and I do it. In other words, I must not allow too much time between the arrival of the opportunity and its execution. Discipline can die in the gap between those two things. Sometimes I keep going simply because I do not allow myself the luxury of quitting.

Sometimes, I find a recovery of discipline by simplifying my life, particularly when I have been trying too hard. When I feel my discipline becoming a tyrant rather than a friend, I intentionally cut back and slow down. I turn the volume down. I know that if I do not de-intensify my life, burnout and depletion will soon follow.

Discipline is difficult to gain and easy to lose. My ways of hanging on to it may not suit you. My point in sharing them is to let you know that I struggle with maintaining discipline just like you do. But I have come to see it as an essential scene in the formation drama. [2]

DIRECTION

Discipline will lead us into the next scene in the drama, direction. I want to treat it as a separate scene, but for many it will be a concrete and meaningful way to maintain discipline. By direction I mean the process of relating to another individual for accountability and growth. Spiritual direction has been practiced in the church for centuries, but to many evangelical Protestants it is a new concept. [3]

To involve yourself in spiritual direction, it is necessary to select another individual to be your director. This is a person who is mature in the faith, someone you trust and feel comfortable and at home with, and who can help you grow in Christlikeness. The person may be an ordained person in whom you have confidence, or a trusted friend. The main thing is that the director not be a novice in the faith.

What occurs in the spiritual direction process is largely up to you, for your own growing edges are the agenda for the relationship. The purpose of the meetings with your director is not therapeutic. That is, it is not a counseling relationship, but is based on finding ways and means to mature, precisely at the points where you sense the greatest potential for growth.

One picture is worth a thousand words, so let me give you an example from my own ministry of spiritual direction. A student and I had covenanted to meet once a month for his spiritual direction. I asked him to come to our first meeting with a list of three or four growing-edge concerns—places where he felt special need or potential for growth. At our first meeting, we agreed that intercession was the main area among the several he listed. For the next several sessions, we talked about intercession, shared our experiences of it, read about other people's practice of it, etc. The outcome was that he discovered a pattern for intercession that fit his personality, his time schedule, and his desires in this dimension of his spiritual life. And once he felt a sense of improvement in this area, we moved on to something else.

The specific process of spiritual direction can vary.[4] The purpose of the experience is to give you someone with whom to share and from whom you can receive valuable insights to help you develop particular aspects of your faith. The disciples went out two by two. Timothy had Paul. In later centuries, Augustine had Ambrose, and John Wesley had his mother, Susannah. We grow best spiritually in fellowship with another Christian. Spiritual direction is one process by which we do that.

The focus of spiritual direction is not on the frequency or duration of the meetings. If you've become accustomed to weekly, small group fellowships, a monthly or quarterly meeting with a spiritual director may not seem often enough. Here you need to remember that the purpose of spiritual direction is different from the weekly fellowship groups. In spiritual direction, the goal is to assess trends in your development, and that takes time. If you stay with some particular aspect of your spiritual formation for a month or longer, you can see how it is shaping up. The meetings you have with your spiritual director can then be devoted to dealing with those aspects of your growth that are most formative in your life.

For this reason, people in spiritual direction usually keep a journal. By entering daily or frequent reflections, they are able to see and assess the larger spiritual trends. The journal is a place for capturing insights that come in between direction sessions. It

is a spiritual data base that will trigger reflection and discussion.[5]
Over a longer period of time it will be a valuable record of your
spiritual maturity.

In this process of spiritual direction, the main thing to
guard against is the loss of your uniqueness. Remember, the goal
of spiritual direction is growth in Christlikeness. Whenever you
sense that you are being squeezed into the mold of your director's preferences, it's probably time to end the relationship. The
main danger in spiritual direction is that the director becomes
more of a dictator than a guide. A director should not want
people to become like him or her, but like Christ. Good direc-
tors will resist the temptation to make directees follow their
paths. By the same token, those who seek direction should be on
the alert for dynamics in the process of direction which are
robbing them of their uniqueness.

When rightly practiced, spiritual direction becomes a
very exciting and meaningful aspect of our spiritual development. We eagerly look forward to the time when we meet with
our director, for we know that such times will provide new and
needed insights for our maturation. It is a time when we can let
our own lives and concerns become the agenda for attention and
discussion. It is a time when we can talk personally and intimate-
ly with a trusted friend, when we can chart some courses for the
future, and be held accountable for staying on them. Spiritual
direction is to the soul what the final, detailed brush strokes are
to a painting. It is the personalizing of the picture which thus
brings out the ultimate beauty.

DEVELOPMENT

Direction leads us to the next scene in the drama, development.
By this I mean the aspect of spiritual formation which will not
allow us to become passively satisfied where we are. Dr. John
Oswalt says that when we cross the line from spiritual death to

spiritual life, we face a great temptation—to see how close to the line we can remain without falling back over. We flirt with sin and live shallow lives. This is tragic, since the purpose in crossing the line is to see how far beyond it we can move with the remaining life we have. True spirituality is the lifelong process of developing that which has come to be real in our lives.

But are we left to develop randomly? By no means! There are many principles and resources to help us grow in positive directions. As you read the pages of this book, you will find areas where development is possible and you'll be given many suggestions to accomplish it. At this point, let me add several that especially help us to flesh out our commitment to discipline.

† First, development should take place at the points of greatest potential. We've already seen that growth is not consistent in all areas of our spiritual life. For example, if we are making particular progress in our use of Scripture, that may be the area to especially develop. It's the spiritual application of the principle, "Strike while the iron is hot."

† Development may take place at points of greatest need. Sometimes the Holy Spirit convicts us that a certain area in our spirituality is not coming along as it should. Such conviction, though uncomfortable, is intended for our enrichment. If we respond and follow through by developing the "weak muscle" in our soul, we find that we have grown in significant ways.

For example, one of the "weak muscles" I have dealt with is my lack of knowledge about the classics of Christian spirituality. Most of us are even hard-pressed to name more than five historic writers and works that deal with the spiritual life. This is evidence of how rootless we are in our spiritual formation. Several years ago, the Holy Spirit convicted me at this very point. And since then, I have kept some devotional classics in my spiritual diet. [6]

† Spiritual development can also take place as we move from one life stage to another. As we pay attention to

our chronological and developmental changes, we can experience profound spiritual growth. I've noticed this most in relationship to marriage. After nearly twenty years with Jeannie and the children, there have been numerous times when I have had to relate my spiritual formation to the fact that I am a husband and father. Both roles have developed and changed over the years, and my spiritual life has had to undergo change as well. Through the Bible and secondary devotional material, I've sought to move from one stage to another with the resources of a sound spirituality.

This kind of development is not jerky and choppy. Instead, it has a feel of naturalness about it. We don't have to "push" anything, for spiritual development is a response to what is going on inside us and around us. We can take a lesson from the athletes who build their bodies at a slow, steady pace. They do not have to accomplish it all today, or even tomorrow. They have time to move toward the goal with considered determination, and they work faithfully, but not feverishly. They ultimately accomplish more with steady consistency than if they were to huff and puff, and jump and jerk their way along.

DEPLOYMENT

Related to the scene of development is that of deployment, for nothing can choke the life out of spiritual life any faster than failing to apply it to the real world. Walter Trobisch calls this lack becoming "spiritually stuffed."[7]

God lives in us in order to live through us. Christ calls us to go into the world and improve the quality of life. Deployment is vitally necessary if we are to keep spiritual formation from deteriorating into a privatized "me and Jesus" experience. Remembering that true faith is always lived out can save us from being caught in spiritual myopia.

Spiritual deployment also links our spirituality with our

vocational pursuits. In the old West, many churches had signs on their front doors, "Check your guns as you enter." On many church doors today is this unwritten message, "Check your vocations as you enter." Too often we ask people to forget for an hour or two that they have professional skills. We almost force them to think in such a way that they never have a chance to apply their faith to where they live and work. This is not true spirituality.

Churches everywhere desperately need to ask the applicational questions. Many Sunday School classes need to know how the faith applies to their members more than they need to study the journeys of Paul again. The greatest hope we have for the influencing of society is as we connect our faith to our vocations and move out into the world to live as committed Christians. Spiritual life is weakened when it is divorced from the daily issues it is intended to address.

Authentic deployment leads to servanthood. But we run from servanthood because we think God is going to throw us immediately into the deep end of the pool. The lesson of Scripture is that God works with us in proportion to our faith. Notice in the Gospels how Jesus worked slowly and gently with the young disciples. At first, He asked them to watch Him. Then He asked them to do a few simple tasks. It was only after Pentecost that they assumed a major role in the Christian enterprise. We can be sure that if God worked with the first disciples that way, He will do the same with us. We do not have to be afraid of serving a loving God who takes our level of maturity into account.

Furthermore, authentic deployment is not an exercise in confusion. Have you ever become overwhelmed with the many needs in the world? Maybe you've caught yourself saying, "How can I know where to begin when there's so much that needs to be done?" That's one of the surest signs that we are not listening to the Holy Spirit. One of the tricks of Satan is to so overwhelm us by the world's needs that we are immobilized.

In his book, *A Testament of Devotion*, Thomas Kelly wrote, "God does not ask you to die on every cross you see."[8] One of the first things the Holy Spirit will do is convince you that the world is too big for you to handle. He will convince you that it is impossible to be substantively involved in every conceivable cause. The Spirit does this in order that you might begin to *focus* on a cause or two in which you can become meaningfully involved and really make a difference.

This kind of deployment will usually occur simultaneously on two levels. First, you select a cause or two close at hand— something you can get involved in personally. But second, you will be moved to select a cause or two (maybe more, depending on your resources) that you can support with your finances. Through this your reach is extended and you are enabled to support those persons who have felt God's call to involve themselves in issues beyond your reach. Spiritual deployment becomes a tailor-made experience of involvement and support that is deeply meaningful and is used by God to get things done.

DELIGHT

The last scene then becomes one of delight. True spirituality creates a depth of delight that can hardly be put into words. But please notice that I did not say that it produces comfort. Counterfeit spiritualities offer that. Delight, however, is that sense of being on the right track even when the track is difficult and the way is hard. To be sure, there will be plenty of times when happiness and comfort are the order of the day. God is not a sadist. But neither is He a Santa Claus. Life is uncertain enough so that we can know our spiritual life will not and cannot be one of ease all the time. Delight is that quality which says as Paul did, "I have learned to be content whatever the circumstance" (Philippians 4:12).

I have a friend named Robert Standhardt. Because of a birth accident, Robert is a quadriplegic. To the average observer, he easily fits the category of a "handicapped person." Sure, Robert has some limitations, but he is not handicapped! Why? Because he has found delight in his spiritual life. Not ease or comfort, but delight. And as a United Methodist minister, he shares that delight with others for their own enrichment. When we're together, he shares it with me.

Robert Standhardt reminds me that true delight is not connected to or dependent upon one's physical condition. If I were to define that delight, I'd call it the inner certainty that out of all the faith options available, we know that through Christ we have found the Way. We are on the road that leads to abundant and everlasting life. That is delightful, and authentic spirituality will lead us to this experience.

And so the curtain comes down on the drama. It has taken two chapters to describe it. And even at that we have only seen descriptive scenes, and have had to hurry along. You may be thinking, "There is so much. I could never do this by myself." Well, the good news is that you do not have to do it by yourself.

PUTTING FEET TO FAITH

He appointed twelve—designating them apostles—
that they might be with Him and that He might send
them out to preach, and to have authority to drive
out demons.   Mark 3:13-15

PRACTICE SILENCE

Consider that Jesus will call you to demonstrate your faith in the world
in concrete ways. Remember that He will never ask you to do this by
yourself or in your own strength.

PRACTICE REFLECTION

Effective action follows from prior discipline. How do you need to
discipline your life to express your faith more effectively?

Do you feel the need for a guide to assist your spiritual
formation? What kind of person do you see as being helpful to you?

PRACTICE RESOLUTION

Decide to become a "maximum" Christian, and see how far you can go.

PRACTICE PRAYER

Praise God for the opportunity of living in intimacy with Him.

PRACTICE READING

Psalm 84 and John 6:53-69

FOUR

NEVER ALONE!

If you're a parent, you have probably heard your children say, "I'll go if you'll go with me" or "I'll go if you'll go first." It may have been a strange place or a dark room that your children would commit themselves to enter, *only if* they knew you would be with them. Children have a correct instinct that new and unfamiliar situations should not be entered into alone.

The possibilities which we have shared in the previous three chapters are exciting and powerful. However, I would not be surprised if you are hesitant to jump right in and begin to make them a part of your life. Like little children, our sensitivities are keen. We know this kind of living cannot be accomplished in the power of our own strength. If we are to live this way, we must have the help of our Heavenly Father.

Ironically, this childlike sensitivity is precisely what Jesus wanted in His disciples. As long as they labored under the notion that they could do it alone, they were not ready for the quality of discipleship and spiritual life which Jesus had in mind. They had to be stripped of self-sufficiency and filled with receptive humility. The days immediately surrounding Jesus' crucifixion brought them to that place. The events of those days showed them how weak they really were, how unprepared to live as Christ's disciples in the world. Like children, they had to know that Christ would be with them in the life and ministry to which He was calling them.

And that is what He promised—"Surely I will be with

you always, to the very end of the age" (Matthew 28:20). This promise was fully actualized on the Day of Pentecost when the Holy Spirit came in power upon the disciples. But even in Christ's words, the disciples found the assurance they needed to go on without His physical presence. They knew that the Christian venture was possible, precisely because He *would* be with them. From that time forward, they would never be alone.

Each of us, if we are to be alive in our walk with God, must be stripped of all notions of self-sufficiency. We must come to the place of realizing that it is " 'not by might nor by power, but by My Spirit,' says the Lord Almighty" (Zechariah 4:6). The power to live the Christian life is not some impersonal force. Rather, it is the presence of the personal Christ. Like the good parent, He never asks us to go without Him into new or unfamiliar territory.

In this chapter, I want to describe the reality of the God who never leaves us alone, something we need to grasp if we are to make progress in our spiritual formation. And we are helped in our understanding through several powerful ideas in Scripture.

GOD GOES BEFORE

The first picture in Scripture is that of the God who goes before us. This idea is so prevalent in the Bible that it is virtually impossible to capture it with a few references. We see it as early as the expulsion of Adam and Eve from the Garden of Eden, when God began to lead this primal family. It continued in God's "going before" the various patriarchs. And it climaxed in the great deliverance of the Israelites from Egypt, as God led them in their journey as a pillar of cloud by day and a pillar of fire by night. In fact, it can be said that the rest of the Old Testament narratives, including the preparation for a Messiah, are examples of the God who goes ahead of us to prepare the way.

With the opening of the New Testament, God used John

the Baptist to prepare the way of the Lord. It was Jesus Himself who led the disciples. He even called Himself the Way and asked people to follow Him. After Christ's resurrection, it was the Holy Spirit who led the apostles individually and the church collectively into new ministries and locations. Certainly the Apostle Paul had a definite sense of being guided throughout the years of his ministry. And in the final book of the Bible, John was led by the risen Christ to experience aspects of history that await the end of the age. In all these incidents, we see the God who goes before.

This is an essential concept for us to grasp in our spiritual formation. If we believe that our days and experiences are haphazard and accidental, we will find it difficult to trust God as He works in our lives. Unless we see the particular pieces of our lives as fitting into a larger picture, we can easily miss a pattern of growth and development. Unless we believe in the God who goes before us, we will cling to the security of the past rather than finding the new directions God desires for us.

Theologians have argued for centuries about the means of this leading. In a practical sense, it does not matter much whether you believe in some kind of predestination or in a less-predetermined manner of guidance. The point in both perspectives is that God is sovereign and in control. He is leading. Your life and mine have plan, purpose, and order. It is God's part to lead; it is our part to follow that leading.

To accept this inevitably means to wrestle with the problem of knowing God's will, of finding out where He wants us to go. Henri Nouwen has helped me in this regard. On one occasion during an interview, when he was asked about the question of knowing God's will, Nouwen commented, "The funny thing in life is that by the time I need to know, I always know. My problem is that I always want to know too soon."[1]

I realize that this is my problem too. I want to be able to see too far down the path. I want to know what my life will be like next year, five years from now, or maybe even at retirement. When I devote too much mental and spiritual energy to this kind of thinking, I fail to see God's leading in the present—this moment or this day. Someone has said that God has intentionally divided life up into day-size portions, and that we should learn to live within those portions.

This does not mean that we are to be totally unconcerned about the future. The Bible nowhere describes Christians as people who fail to plan or prepare themselves. But it does show them to be people who do not so plan their own futures that they are inflexible. We are not to live so much in the future that we lose the opportunities of the present.

The God who goes before us invites us to trust Him for the future. When we do, we are liberated to live in the present. We are freed to focus our spiritual energies on the things immediately before us, and to live with a greater single-mindedness.

As a child I would often take a magnifying glass outside on a sunny day, especially in the fall when the dry leaves were on the ground. I would make a little pile of leaves and then hold my magnifying glass toward the sun, focusing it until a concentrated beam of light started a fire. It was amazing to see how focused that light could become, and how, as it became more focused, it had more power.

Our lives are like that. We multiply our power when we focus our attention on situations in front of us, and leave the larger future to the God who goes before us. We lose power by being too spread out—"worried and upset about many things" (Luke 10:41). Spiritual formation is not unrelated to good time-management principles which enable us to so order our lives that we can give fuller attention to the tasks of today.[2] But underneath the techniques of time management must be the confidence that we can, in fact, surrender our tomorrows to the God who is out ahead of us leading and guiding.

GOD STANDS BESIDE

It is not enough, however, to acknowledge the God who goes before us. We need another image burned into our minds and hearts, of the God who stands beside us. The God of the future becomes the God of the present. The Leader becomes the Enabler.

† One of the traditions which enriched the spirituality of John Wesley was Puritanism, the tradition in which both of his parents were brought up. The Puritans spoke of the events of life as "God moments." They believed that there was never a moment when God was not present with them for guidance, comfort, and strength. The challenge of the spiritual life was to live with an increasing consciousness of this fact.

Such "God moments" are based on a deeper understanding of time. In the Bible there are two Greek words for time, *chronos* and *kairos*. Chronos time is the chronological, sequential passage of time. It includes seconds, minutes, hours, days. Kairos time is time within time. We could describe it as the presence and activity of God in the midst of our time. It is a quality in the midst of quantity. As Christians, we believe that our lives (chronos) can be lived as God's presence (kairos) fills and guides our actions. In fact, one definition of spiritual formation—the life of God in the soul of man—implies a harmonization of the chronos and kairos dimensions of time.

This idea has frequently been illustrated through the life of Brother Lawrence, a sixteenth-century monastic who served his fellow monks and the Lord by washing dishes in the monastery kitchen.[3] He testified that he came to the place in his spiritual life where the presence of God was as real to him in the kitchen as it was in the cathedral. He grew in his ability to sense the presence of God throughout the day. In the twentieth century, this same idea has been communicated by the Quaker writer, Thomas Kelly, who maintains that we have been created to live on two levels at once—being fully engaged in the affairs of life, but at the same time in communion with God. [4]

Admittedly, this kind of living is not easy, and we will struggle with it all our lives. But the reality of the God who stands beside us makes it possible. In our spiritual formation, we are closing the gaps in the day between the times when we are aware of God's nearness. In the beginning, we may let hours go by without connecting the chronos and kairos. But as we continue to give ourselves to this discipline, the gap between the two will become narrower.

† If we are to seek for this kind of harmonization in life, it is legitimate to ask, "What are the benefits of recognizing the God who stands beside us?" One of the best places to go for an answer is Ephesians 6:10-18, a passage in which Paul speaks about living in the strength of the Lord. To show how this is done, he uses the clothing of a Roman soldier to show how the power of God is variously available to us. Each piece of clothing depicts another way in which the presence of God enables us to live with power and purpose. [5] God comes into the days of our lives to equip us to meet and overcome the pressures and problems we face.

But the benefits of knowing the God who is near are greater than simply the enabling qualities which He gives. God does not stand beside us simply to make us successful. He stands beside us to provide a deep sense of communion. And it is a communion that exists in every circumstance of life. We see this in Psalm 23 where David writes, "Yea, though I walk through the valley of the shadow of death, I will fear no evil; for You are with me" (NKJV). Committing our ways to the God who stands beside us is our witness that the strength and presence of God are adequate, even when we do not succeed—even when life does not treat us fairly.

One of the problems in contemporary Christianity is the success syndrome—the message that if you have God, you'll be a winner. Cast in this light, God becomes a utilitarian deity, useful to help us get ahead and even to prosper materially. While such a being is handy to have around, it is also shallow, and a dim reflection of the God who stands beside us.

I'm thankful that Dr. Leighton Ford has written the book which describes his son's sudden death during heart surgery.[6] He pulls no punches in showing how this kind of loss is soul-wrenching. Even years later it is not easy for him to go places where Sandy used to go. But the final word is that the God who is near is the God who is able—able to sustain us even in the face of tragedy and grief.

The God who stands beside us does so on the good days and the bad. He is near when we succeed and when we fail. He is with us when we prosper and when we hurt. The circumstances of our lives are not the indicators of His presence or His love. For us to commit ourselves to the ongoing process of spiritual formation, we must know that He is with us in the present. And we must also be certain that His presence is not capricious, but rather that it is consistent and continual, reaching beyond all time.

GOD DWELLS WITHIN

As powerful as the images of leading and enabling are, there is a third picture that rounds out our understanding of the ministry of God in our lives. It is the God who dwells within us. The deepest truth in the Christian faith is that God not only wants to influence us, but also wants to infill us. This is what Jesus was telling the disciples when He said that the Holy Spirit would be in them (John 14:17).

When I became a Christian over twenty years ago, I marveled at the words of Christ in Revelation 3:20: "Behold, I stand at the door and knock. If anyone hears My voice and opens the door, I will come to him and dine with him, and he with Me"

(NKJV). I could scarcely comprehend the thought that the living Christ was able and willing to live in my life. This entirely new understanding of Christianity transformed faith from being primarily propositional to being profoundly personal. Admittedly, there is deep mystery here—one that I understand less now than I did at the beginning. But I am more committed to a personal Christianity than ever before. For as the mystery has grown in size, it has also increased in potency.

We have noted already that the idea of "in Christ" and "Christ in you" is perhaps the most powerful image in all of Scripture to describe the Christian life; yet the question remains, "Why does God desire this degree of intimacy and closeness with us?" God's actions are always for a purpose. As I have considered the purposes of God with respect to our being indwelt by the Spirit, the following ideas stand out in my mind.

† The first is our need for purification. When God moves into our lives, it is with the intention of cleaning out the impurities which cause us to think, act, and speak contrary to the divine will for our lives. I've always been intrigued by Peter's declaration when he first realized who Jesus was. He found himself in the presence of the Son of God and cried out, "Depart from me, for I am a sinful man, O Lord!" (Luke 5:8, NKJV) Jesus had not said a word about Peter's sinfulness, but somehow His presence made it apparent.

It should not surprise us that God's first action within is to cleanse us. It is His intention to live in our lives, so it only stands to reason that He will want to make for Himself a fit dwelling place. When Jeannie and I bought a new home, our first action was to go through the house, room by room, cleaning and preparing it for occupancy. We wanted the home to reflect the lifestyle of our family. So too in the spiritual life, it is God's first desire that we reflect the character of the One who now lives inside. This changes the idea of purification from a negative one to a positive one.

The renewing and cleansing activity of God is based on two great truths: that we are sinful and in need of such cleansing, and that we are improvable through the working of God's grace in our lives. The first truth states the fact, the second describes the potential. E. Stanley Jones put it this way, "Left to yourself, you're a problem. But left to God, you're a possibility!"[7]

This means that the indwelling God is an active presence in our lives. His entrance may provide substantial and even dramatic changes, but we will always sense a continuing work which "fine tunes" even that which He now lives in. If you have ever watched a teenager polish and shine his car for hours, you have some idea of the attention and care which our Heavenly Father gives to us. It seems that God never tires of adding those special touches of His love and grace which make us more and more like Himself.

The wonder is that this purification can work with the past as well as with the present.[8] Through the Spirit, God is able to penetrate our subconscious and liberate us from every obstacle which prevents us from reflecting His glory. Freedom from the past makes possible a more powerful present and creates greater hope that our tomorrows are not outside the reach of God's renewing abilities.

This dimension of God's indwelling presence ministered powerfully to me at a time when I became aware of my explosive temper. It was only after getting married that I realized I had this problem, and ironically, Jeannie was usually the target of my anger. I was shocked by this and very much afraid, for I knew I could not continue to love her as I should and have an explosive temper. It all came to a climax one afternoon as the Holy Spirit helped me examine my life from the past to the present. New things came to light as God started the process of healing this great need in my life. The healing was not fully completed that day, but God broke the back of my temper and gave me new hope for the future.

† This indwelling presence also provides us with power. I could think of no greater tragedy than to have the presence of God in our lives, but yet be unable to fulfill His desires for us. The mere fact that God gives power is proof that we need it if we are to live the Christian life. God's offer of power is the ultimate proof that we are not self-sufficient.

As I write these words, we are experiencing a terrible winter blizzard. Just two days ago it was a lovely Indian summer, but now the winds are beating against our home and the temperature has dropped forty degrees! Even our dog has noticed the change. In a word, it's cold! But our home is warm and comfortable, thanks to the heat pump. The house cannot warm itself, so built into it is a heating unit specifically designed to provide the much needed warmth.

In like manner, I cannot live the Christian life in my own strength. With so many self-help and self-improvement programs around today, I'm convinced it is extremely difficult to overcome the tendency toward self-reliance. But overcome it we must if we are to experience the totality of God's work in our lives. I like the way *The Living Bible* translates 2 Corinthians 4:7, "Everyone can see that the glorious power within must be from God and is not our own."

Robert Boyd Munger has written a little booklet which has become a devotional classic, "My Heart, Christ's Home." It is a story of Christ coming into a house with many rooms, each room signifying a dimension of life. One represents the work which we do—the workroom. When Christ enters, He asks the person to show Him what is being accomplished. The person replies that he has done some things, but is still frustrated with feelings of helplessness. To this Christ replies, "Let Me help you." He moves over to the workbench and slips His hands underneath the person's, and with the powerful hands of Christ guiding and enabling the person's hands, new and wonderful things are accomplished. [9]

This is the kind of power we're talking about. It is not that God sets our gifts and graces aside and works without us. No, He comes to work *with* our strengths and abilities, enabling us by His power to accomplish more than we ever could alone. We begin to live with a sense that our ideas and actions are being generated by another Source. We can say with Paul, "It is no longer I who live, but Christ lives in me" (Galatians 2:20).

† This leads us to a third gift from the indwelling God, perspective. Having experienced the ongoing purification of God and realized that His power is at work within us, we are given a new perspective on ourselves and on life. This is what Jesus was talking about when He said that people needed to have "eyes to see" and "ears to hear." We need to view life from a Christian perspective.

I've often thought that the greatest need in the church is for Christians to live like Christians. I agree with Dr. William Willimon, Dean of the Chapel at Duke University, who says that the greatest need in Christianity today is for "Christians to be who they are."[10] We too easily adopt the thought and behavior patterns of our secularized age, and then coat a thin layer of "faith" over it in an attempt to legitimize what we do. We come dangerously close to fulfilling Leslie Weatherhead's observation that the only thing wrong with Christianity is that it has never really been tried.[11]

We desperately need to understand that the fundamental definition of our life is "Christian." Too often we define ourselves by what we do; we say we are doctors, teachers, accountants, homemakers, etc. But function never defines our personhood. Instead, *we are defined by who we are.* Once this idea really captures us, we will begin to be the agents of witness and renewal which our Lord intends for us to be.

Charles M. Sheldon's *In His Steps* is the story of a town that was transformed by people asking the question, "What would Jesus do?"[12] Some have criticized Sheldon's book as an oversimplification of Christian behavior. And while it is true that this question alone is not the sum total of how we shape our actions, it would go a long way in helping us regain a Christian perspective on life.

Through these three images we've seen that God's presence and activity in our lives is comprehensive. As Leader, Enabler, and Infiller, He provides for the totality of our needs. As He goes ahead, stands beside, and lives within, we discover both the depth and intimacy of our relationship with God. He never intended for us to live the Christian life by ourselves or in our own strength. No matter where we are or what we face, we are never alone!

THE ALL-SUFFICIENT GOD

My God will meet all your needs according to His glorious riches in Christ Jesus.   Philippians 4:19

PRACTICE SILENCE

Think about times when you've experienced the God who goes before, the God who stands beside, and the God who dwells within.

PRACTICE REFLECTION

It is normal to prefer one portrayal of God. Of the three described in this chapter, do you have a preference? Why?

Our preferences may be reflections of our *needs*. Does your preference serve as an avenue through which He can minister to your needs? Do you need to develop your faith along some new lines?

PRACTICE RESOLUTION

Allow God to search through your life, reveal the needs He chooses to explore, and meet them in His time and in His way.

PRACTICE PRAYER

Write a prayer of thanksgiving that God is always active in your life.

PRACTICE READING

Psalm 139:1-14 and Philippians 4:11-13

FIVE

A NEW WAY TO LIVE

On one occasion I was meeting with a group which was responsible for developing spiritual formation materials for their denomination. As the discussion progressed, someone said, "Steve, if I hear what you're saying, then spiritual formation cannot be thought of as a program." For that person and the group, this was a difficult thing to grasp. All of us are so inclined to think of programs, plans, and procedures that it is not easy to see that spiritual formation can never be captured or described in this way. Instead, we are challenged to understand spiritual formation as a total lifestyle—indeed, a new way to live.

Spiritual formation is not something you can package. It is not another self-help program. It cannot be described as "Ninety days to a new you." In fact, spiritual formation does not think in terms of beginnings and endings. It thinks in terms of the totality of life. In this chapter we want to see how this is so.

THEOLOGY

We begin with a theology. Undergirding spiritual formation is the affirmation, "Jesus is Lord!" This was the earliest creed of Christianity, and it is the benchmark for contemporary spiritual formation. Why? Because it underscores the fact that "in Christ" life can no longer be understood in terms of categories and compartments. Every second of my day and every area of my life come under His lordship.

E. Stanley Jones frequently reminded people, "He must be God of all or not God at all."¹ This is not difficult to see logically, but it is hard to put into practice existentially. We know it, but we have trouble living it. There are two kinds of atheists. The first believes God does not exist. The second lives as if He did not exist. Ironically, both roads end up at the same place. God is pushed to the fringes of life, or out of the picture altogether. In our time, the second category of atheism is the greater danger. As society becomes more secularized and technological potential increases, the human temptation is to view God as irrelevant.

Several years ago I had the opportunity to hear a NASA scientist speak about the space program. He was a professing Christian, and in the middle of his address he made this interesting comment, "One of our tendencies in science is to blame God when something goes wrong, and to pat ourselves on the back when it goes right." For me, this remark captured the contemporary, secular spirit that is quick to heap praise on itself, but equally quick to look for a scapegoat when things go wrong. As long as our technology serves us, it is especially easy to consign God to a place of relative insignificance.

To remind ourselves that "Jesus is Lord" is to take the first critical step toward the kind of spiritual formation we've been describing. It is the step which we see the saints of the ages taking, for they simply did not think in compartmentalized fashion as we do today. Life for them was unitive and whole. God was the all-pervasive presence in the world. They knew the reality Paul was communicating about Christ when he wrote, "In Him all things hold together" (Colossians 1:17).

Consequently, they sought a lifestyle which would reflect and affirm their theology. They were trying to fulfill the Scripture which told them to "take captive every thought to make it obedient to Christ" (2 Corinthians 10:5). To be sure, some of their practices were exotic and excessive, but their intention was to live a life of unbroken fellowship with God through Christ. Theirs was a conscious application of their belief that "Jesus is Lord."

RHYTHM

If this theological affirmation is the underpinning of spiritual formation, then we will seek for ways to apply it to our lives. We need to move beyond the mere statement of belief in Christ's lordship to ways and means of expressing that in our daily living. One of the first steps is to regain a sense of rhythm in our living. In the industrialized West, we are so production-oriented that we have all but lost this concept. But if spiritual formation is to be our way of life, we must regain contact with this vital element.

† This rhythm is reflected in Jesus' words to His disciples, "Come with Me by yourselves to a quiet place and get some rest" (Mark 6:31). A few years ago it dawned on me that this phrase is as truly in the Bible as any of the work-oriented passages, and that Jesus expects me to fulfill this just as much as He expects me to live in harmony with any other Scripture.

The context of these words is insightful, for the preceding verse tells us that Jesus and the disciples had been so busy they had not even had time to eat. Sound familiar? Does going at full steam describe your pace much of the time? If so, notice what Jesus did. Right in the middle of the pressure, He put on the brakes. He broke away from the frenzied activity and took His disciples to a solitary place.

On surface examination, we draw back. After all, how could Jesus leave genuine need and take a break? But asking such a question reveals how far we are from the biblical perspective. Jesus' decision was a deep expression of the principle of action/reflection which is built into the fabric of life. Furthermore, it was an expression of the way Jesus Himself lived.

Go all the way back into the Creation story. Six days

God labored, but on the seventh day He rested. As the nation of Israel came into existence, the people were commanded to discover and express this same rhythm in their lives. When Jesus came on the scene, He was a walking demonstration of life in balance. On many occasions He withdrew to pray. The Gospels show us several times when the disciples could not find Him because He was preferring solitude to the group or the crowd. Yet never once is there the slightest hint that by doing so He was unconcerned about the needs of others. On the contrary, times of solitude made Him more ready for life's demands than He would have been, had He measured accomplishment by the amount of work turned out.

My friend and colleague Dr. Donald Demaray tells a story which graphically illustrates this truth. He was attending a meeting where E. Stanley Jones was speaking. Don determined that he would not leave the conference without visiting with Brother Stanley. After one of the sessions, he went to Dr. Jones' room in the hotel and knocked on the door. There was no answer. Certain that Stanley Jones was in his room, Don knocked again—a bit louder. Still there was no answer. Disappointed, Don went on his way. Later when he finally made contact with Brother Stanley he asked him, "Didn't you hear a knock at your door this afternoon?" "Of course," replied Dr. Jones, "but I have learned that if a person is available to everyone, he will become no good to anyone."

Ironically, what we as Christians have forgotten is now being emphasized by contemporary management theorists. Nearly every book on management I've read urges the manager to schedule time each day for personal reflection and enrichment. The truth is that we work better and work more efficiently when we take time for solitude and silence. Spiritual formation, while not defining its goal in terms of increased efficiency, is trying to bring us back to the place of viewing life rhythmically, so that we balance action with reflection.

† Related to this is the rhythm of community and solitude. Most of us live out our days in the midst of crowds. Whether in factories, office buildings, or even at home, we find ourselves almost continually in the presence of others. Some people think they have to be in a crowd to feel happy. While people are God-given gifts to enrich us, they can drain our spiritual life.

This need for solitude in the midst of community was underlined for me when I heard Richard Foster say that some of us need to "fast from people."[2] We normally think of fasting as abstaining from food, but Dr. Foster said that many of us need to fast from people and rediscover the art of being alone. To be continually in the presence of people is to lose the art of communing with our own soul. People can distract us from the yearnings of our own hearts. We can become so immersed in others that we lose touch with ourselves.

I've discovered this need through marriage. My wife, Jeannie, has finally gotten through to me with the message that she needs space in our relationship. For too long, I thought that whenever I had an opportunity, I needed to be with her. What I didn't realize was that in so doing, I was actually smothering her, and robbing us both of precious time to be alone with our own thoughts. I now know that part of my overattention was an insecurity, a fear that if I was not in her life as much as possible, she might become interested in someone or something else. I have come to see that our relationship is actually strengthened as each of us allows the other to have times of solitude.

† There's another dimension of this rhythm which needs to be mentioned—that of humor and sobriety.[3] Thomas Merton once said, "The mark of a saint is the ability to laugh." That was his way of saying that most of us take ourselves far too seriously. Overdosing on sobriety can easily create feelings of indispensability, and convince us that everything has to be done "now." This puts tremendous and unrealistic pressure on us and on those around us.

I frequently conduct seminars for ordained ministers. I regard them, on the whole, as professionals who are trying awfully hard to prove their worth. To be sure, part of this attempt is played against the backdrop of a culture in which the clergy is often viewed as irrelevant. But this frenzied effort at self-justification can create a somber and overserious response to life. To try to loosen them up, I tell them, "I can prove that you are not indispensable. It's simple. Just die, and within a couple of weeks, the church that 'can't do without you' will have found another leader." For a moment there is silence, and then some snickers, as together we realize how we blow our significance all out of proportion. I'm sure the same applies to other professional groups as well.

Why have writers like Erma Bombeck become so popular? I think it's their knack for taking a realistic look at life, and then standing back and laughing at it. We buy their books because we want to know how to do this too. We need their help in seeing the humor that is all around us. They enable us to take life less seriously. And when we read their writings, we find a healthy, cathartic experience taking place deep within us. We feel "cleaned out" by laughing at ourselves and our experiences.

Our tendency to be overly serious is one reason why it is important to have some kind of hobby. It should be a pastime we can enjoy while flubbing up at the same time. When a hobby takes on the character of another serious endeavor, the fun is sapped out of it. As a golfer, I have always been amazed at the number of people who take golf so seriously they cannot enjoy it. To lose the joy of any hobby is the surest sign it is time to find another one.

Spiritual formation invites us to blend and balance humor and sobriety. It calls us to take ourselves less seriously, to pull the plug on stress, and to find enjoyable outlets which remind us of our imperfections but at the same time provide pleasure and relaxation. Coupled with the rhythms of action/reflection and community/solitude, the rhythm of humor/sobriety brings a necessary balance and perspective to life.

GOD-CONSCIOUSNESS

Another major step in this new way of living involves our coming to see spiritual formation more as a life to be lived than a time to be set aside for God. Many of us in evangelical circles cut our spiritual teeth on the practice of Quiet Time. Entire discipleship and accountability systems were developed based on it. Group leaders were trained to ask members, "How's your Quiet Time?" If the answer was positive, it was assumed that the member's spiritual life was in good shape.

Those of us who were nurtured this way know now (and suspected then) that this is too narrow an understanding of spirituality. Grateful as I am for the value of the Quiet Time, I now realize that when wrongly used it can lead to a false compartmentalization of the spiritual life so that we make artificial distinctions between "spiritual" and "secular" life. We can too narrowly focus our time with God on a comparatively few minutes in the day, forgetting that the rest of the day should be lived in God's presence also.

This is not the fault of the Quiet Time method so much as it is the fault of those who teach it and use it. Spiritual formation also includes an emphasis on a specific devotional period or periods in the day. But spiritual formation will not allow us to equate that time with the entirety of our spiritual life.

As I teach my students, I explain it this way, "God does not call you to have a devotional time, but to live a devotional life." This statement assumes the need for specific times of devotion, but expands the spiritual life to include the entire day. I believe this is a logical follow-through on the theology of Jesus' lordship. Jesus lays claim to the totality of my life, not just the corners. The goal of a Quiet Time is to enable me to see, hear, and respond to Christ in all my waking moments.

The goal of spiritual development is to put more and more of our lives in the hands of God, and to see increasingly the activity of God in our lives. Few of us will ever come to the place of unbroken communion, for we are too easily distracted by the things that happen to us. But moving from a time-centered to a life-centered spirituality helps us close the gaps between our moments of God-consciousness.

As good as this is, there is a danger to be avoided. It is the danger of thinking or saying, "Well, I live in the presence of God all day long, so I don't really need to take special time out for devotions." Such an attitude is dangerous and totally misses the point. Just imagine what would happen to a chef in a restaurant who said, "I don't need to take time to eat—I live and work around food all day long." In our spiritual formation, we must set aside definite time in the day so that our souls are nourished consciously and intentionally. But having done that, we should expand our spirituality to include the whole of the day.

This will mean that we capture the spiritual value of the ordinary time in our lives.[4] All of us do pretty well in sensing the presence of God in the big events of life, but we can very easily miss Him in the routine, lackluster moments. One problem of "celebrity Christianity" is that it leaves us with the impression that God dwells only in the spectacular dimensions of life. And that leaves most of us out, for we are ordinary people. Our spiritual formation is dependent upon seeing and responding to God in the ordinary, expected, and often-repeated events of our days.

One of my most vivid memories from childhood is of my dad taking me to our local fire station on Saturday, so that I could play on the trucks. While I dreamed of becoming the world's greatest fireman, my dad just stood by quietly and watched. Now that I'm a father, I know that there were many other ways he could have spent his time. But by being with me, he was saying, "Son, you are worth spending time with." Years later, events like that still live in my mind.

I suspect there is nothing some parents dislike more than diaper changing. It's a job I've heard some "macho men" swear they'd never do. It's not fun, and in a way it feels degrading. But seen with another set of eyes, it can be a profound spiritual experience, for it is a time to serve the most basic needs of a loved child who is helpless to care for himself. When viewed from this perspective, the changing table is transformed into a place of worship, for God is present in this occasion of selfless love.

How many "ordinary times" come to your mind? We all have them. The secret is first to see them, and then to see through them to God. Such times may include jobs we say we'll scream if we have to do one more time. Such tense moments are like a tightrope—we can fall off on either side. If we fall off on one side, we will become negative, critical, even bitter. But if by the grace of God, we land on the other, we will see even these ordinary events as part of the total fabric of God's will in the midst of our lives. And this is essential if we are to move beyond a narrow view of spiritual formation to one that expresses the fullness of God in our days.

VOCATION

A fourth aspect of spiritual living is in knowing the sacredness of your vocation. This is especially necessary in a time when the meaning of work is changing in our society. For many people, work has become more a means of financial gain than of personal fulfillment, and they simply do not view their work as a means of receiving and expressing spiritual life.

The word *vocation* means "to call," and comes from the same root as the word *vocal*. When applied to our work, vocation implies that what we do is the result of someone calling us to do it. And for Christians, that "someone" is God. Ideally, our work should be the result of God's call to apply ourselves, our gifts, and our energies at a particular place in the world.[5]

The word *job* speaks more of a task, a duty, or an obligation, and a step below the idea of vocation. But to work year after year at a job rather than a vocation is to drain our work of the spiritual dimension God intended it to have.

This has several unfortunate results. For one thing, there is a significant spiritual vacuum in every day. From seven to eight hours a day, we have no conscious connection between work and faith, and that is devastating. Another result is that we can assume that only church-related work is truly spiritual. So the laity either comes to assume a second-class status in relation to the clergy, or tries to cram as much church work into their schedules as possible to convince themselves that they are doing something for God.

The new life which spiritual formation calls for invites a person to consider work as an expression of spirituality. Vocation does not require that one's work be fulfilling, easy, or even fair. What it does ask is that we look at it as a means of encountering God and as a means of serving Him. Our daily work is a prime place to express the fruit of the Spirit: love, joy, peace, patience, kindness, goodness, faithfulness, gentleness, and self-control. It is a place to treat other people as people, and to make a contribution to the overall good of humanity.

Spiritual formation challenges us to do our work in this mind-set, if at all possible. And if we come to the conclusion that our job simply does not allow for this to be done, then it may be time to ask whether or not we have heard God's call to the work we are doing. Some may have to reconsider that call if their job is to become a true vocation. A significant part of our spiritual formation is drawing work into the total picture of spiritual life.

This kind of spirituality is not something that happens

automatically. It requires a new rhythm, a new understanding of life, and a new view of vocation. Such realignment of life is not easy. Jesus called it entering upon a narrow way that relatively few would find. But that's not because it is hard to find. It is right in front of us all the time. The irony is that we can be right in the middle of it and still miss it. However, Jesus said that with a new set of eyes and ears, we could come to view life in this new way and enter fully into it. Lord, may it be so!

NEW IS BETTER

Therefore, if anyone is in Christ, he is a new creation; the old has gone; the new has come!

2 Corinthians 5:17

PRACTICE SILENCE

Think about any new ideas which have come to you in the course of reading this book.

PRACTICE REFLECTION

A fascination with newness is not in itself a mark of spirituality. New insights are always to connect with historic biblical truths.

The rhythms described in this chapter help us get in touch with biblical patterns for living. Which rhythm is most productive in your life right now? Which is most needed?

PRACTICE RESOLUTION

Determine by the grace of God to eliminate barriers in your life which keep faith confined and compartmentalized.

PRACTICE PRAYER

Offer the work you do as a point of integration of your faith.

PRACTICE READING

Psalm 15 and Colossians 3:17

S I X

PREPARATION FOR THE JOURNEY

I belong to a travel club connected with one of my credit cards. Among their services is assistance in trip preparation. They will mark the best route for a trip, suggest accommodations, and point out enjoyable places to see along the way. They know that adequate preparation is a necessary prerequisite for a satisfying journey.

On my first extended trip overseas by myself, I had failed to plan for the purchase of gifts and souvenirs. This meant that I had to buy an additional piece of luggage for my return trip, and that additional piece made it nearly impossible for me to carry all my belongings. On the last day of my trip, I had to carry everything half a mile from my lodging to the subway. You can be sure that all the way I was planning how to do it better the next time!

Preparation is important in spiritual formation as well, since this is not something we can simply enter into and expect to master automatically. We can greatly enhance our journey of spiritual development as we prepare ourselves for it by the acquisition of certain attitudes and the practicing of key actions. We want to examine these in this chapter.

RECEPTIVITY

Because spiritual formation originates in the mind and heart, we begin with attitudes. Henri Nouwen has referred to the spiritual life as "paying attention."[1] The assumption underneath this is that God is speaking and acting in our lives. If we are to be formed by His revelation, we must be receptive to Him. Such attentiveness is not passive but active. It consciously participates in the divine drama by looking for evidences of God's presence.

I'm afraid this ability has been dulled by television. Some of you will be able to remember with me the joy of listening to the old radio programs. One of my earliest memories is sitting with my parents listening to such shows as *Amos and Andy* and *The Lone Ranger*. Radio made us active participants. We had to create the scenes and the characters.

By contrast, television makes us passive observers. Once *Amos and Andy* and *The Lone Ranger* were televised, everyone knew what the characters looked like, and they looked alike to everyone. We no longer had to create them in our minds. We merely watched. If we passively watch for dozens to hundreds of hours each month, a vitally necessary element declines within us—the ability to really pay attention.

Consequently, the media experts have learned how to package their ads in thirty-second and one-minute segments. Even the nightly news broadcasts rarely devote more than three minutes to any single story. The longer shows are little more than a string of fast-moving scenes, each of which lasts for a relatively brief period of time. We have become media-conditioned to expect short bursts of information and entertainment, and we are easily bored when things take longer to unfold and develop.

Spirituality demands that we pay attention and look beneath the surface events of our day to trace the presence of God. For many of us, this will require some retooling. We will have to begin by admitting that we've become too dulled to life. We've been so influenced by our age that we think of life as a blurry series of disconnected events which pass by us day after day. We act and react to these events in robotic fashion. Our first step will be to change from passive to active observers.

We can begin to do this by selecting a single event and asking, "Where was God in that?" And we continue as we include more and more of life under the surveillance of that question. People in Jesus' day also had trouble discerning His presence and activity, and He had to remind them that He was in the ordinary situations of everyday living, even in places where they might not expect Him to be (Matthew 25:31-46).

REFLECTION

Our receptivity needs to be joined to reflection. Receiving increases our powers of observation. Reflecting calls us to interpret what we have observed. Receiving provides the revelatory event. Reflecting takes us around that event to see it from a number of vantage points. Here is where the questions of Who? What? When? Where? Why? and How? can help us. Reflection is holding a diamond up to the light, and turning it in order to see the various colors which its prisms separate.

Let's take a concrete example. My family and I attended our church's annual picnic. It was a time of feasting, fun, and fellowship. Over a hundred people were there representing all ages and relationships. When I looked back on that event and asked, "Where was God in the picnic?" the data came flowing in thick and fast. He was present in those moments when we forgot status and race and class and were simply "one in Christ." He was with us as we forgot generational differences and played games that put children and adults together. He was with us as we met new people and expanded our friendships in the body of Christ.

Reflection enables us to take events big and small and to pay attention to them. Some of us may choose to record our reflections in a journal or notebook. But what really matters is that the reflections make an impression on us. We will each have to find the best means of allowing those impressions to enter, but enter they must if we are to grow spiritually. The revelations of God are not given simply for enjoyment, but also for employment.

Some means of conscious recording of our reflections enables us to go back and remember the specific ways God has been at work in our lives. I know a person who has kept a spiritual journal for years. What he now has is the historic record of the acts of God in his life for over a decade. As he goes back and reads through this material, the events come alive to him, for they are fresh reminders of the reality of God. Without such a means of recording, he would have lost most of this data beneath the sea of consciousness.

RESPONSE

God's revelation is intended to lead us to an appropriate response. That is genuine formation. We are actually changed, shaped, and directed by what we see and hear. In fact, I would argue that every revelation is given for some intended response. It may be the development of a new idea or belief, or the beginning of a new action. Response is at the heart of our spiritual life: it is the demonstration that we are meaningfully engaged in our relationship with God.

Attitude formation is part of our essential preparation for spiritual formation. It is the development of a perspective on life that informs and forms the way we live. I believe this is part of what Paul meant when he called on the Philippian Christians to have "the mind of Christ." We are likewise called to develop attitudes which will enable us to know God and to live for Him.

But attitudes alone are insufficient preparation. We must connect them with concrete actions that give substance and expression to the attitudes. Certain ways to express these attitudes are called *spiritual disciplines*. Others refer to them as *means of grace*. But whatever you call them, they are the specific acts of devotion which enable us to live the life of faith. In what follows, I want to use an historic concept in spiritual formation to describe these actions. The concept is called the Ladder of Devotion.

A ladder suggests movement and progression. Each rung in the ladder corresponds to a specific discipline or action, the use of which enables us to rise higher in the spiritual life. I would not argue in this description for any hierarchy of actions. More to my point is the idea that specific actions contribute to growth. And it is growth that we are after in spiritual formation.

† We begin with the discipline called spiritual reading. In many sources you will find it called by its Latin name, *lectio divina*. Most often it is related to the reading of Scripture, but it can be used with other materials. From the beginning of Christianity, the Holy Bible has been recognized as the primary and normative source for faith and practice. Martin Luther spoke of the necessity of knowing Scripture, "You must know that the Holy Scriptures is a book that makes foolishness of the wisdom of all other books, because none of them teaches eternal life, only this one alone."[2]

Spiritual reading differs from what we might call casual reading. Its quality is not to be equated with quantity. It is not the same as the reading of news magazines, professional journals, or family publications. Dr. Susan Muto describes it as "the kind of reading that can console us in sorrow, deepen our joy, prompt a transformation, orient our whole being toward the Divine. It is the kind of reading, in other words, that nourishes the life of the spirit."[3]

Such reading calls for a shift in perspective. Its goal is not information, but formation. While we will inevitably use sound methodologies and study techniques, and will increase in knowledge, these are not the primary focus of spiritual reading. Our goal is transformation. Key words to guide our spiritual reading are *quality, depth, submission,* and *reflection.*[4] Our purpose is not to ultimately master the text, but rather allow it to master us.

Thomas Merton referred to this kind of reading as "dangerous," because it calls for us to lay our lives open before the Word of God; when we do, we can have unexpected experiences.[5] Such experiences, however, are not to be feared, for they are of a cleansing, renewing, and deepening nature. The unexpected dimension is to find, while we read, that the Word has touched our very soul.

I hope this brief introduction has made spiritual reading appealing. But likely it will require some description of the basic steps in the process. The first is a *prayer for illumination* in which we ask God to speak through the Word which we are about to read. The prayer is short and simple, but it is an expression of deep desire to allow the Bible to come alive in us.

The second step is *unhurried, systematic reading* of the text. This text is usually Scripture, but can also be devotional works as well. It is unhurried because we are not trying to "make it through" in any predetermined amount of time. The goal is encounter, and we are willing to read until we know that we have met God. Some days this will include several chapters of the Bible, but on other days it may be only a few verses. We are not precommitted to any set amount. We are precommitted to searching for God Himself, and this creates a relaxed, unhurried spirit.

Spiritual formation emphasizes systematic reading for the simple reason that this is how the Bible was written. Each book has a beginning and it moves progressively toward its end. Systematic reading does not mean a Genesis to Revelation approach so much as it means selecting a book and reading it from start to finish. In this way we have a better chance of getting into the flow of the material.

The third step leads us to a *sense of discovery*. We ask as we read, "What is the main truth which is being communicated here?" Here is where *lectio divina* is connected with serious study.

There can be no formative reading of the Bible apart from knowledgeable reading. In fact, it is our study which keeps us from finding things in the Bible which aren't there. Anyone who sets out to practice spiritual reading will likewise commit himself or herself to being a good student of the Word.[6]

When we have stated in a sentence or two what the main point of the passage is, we can ask, "How does this truth touch my life?" Perhaps there is a promise to claim, or a warning of something to avoid. We may find a principle to apply to our lives, or a story or parable that will serve as a needed model. Discovery takes us through the historic, literal meaning of the text to the personal, applied meaning of it. Many people like to keep a journal or notebook handy to record these life-impacting statements.

The fourth step of spiritual reading leads us beyond discovery to *application*. We do not leave our time of reading without asking, "How can I begin to put this into practice in my life?" Here too, the journal is a medium for recording our decisions and resolutions. And it becomes a source for reflection at a later time. Through spiritual reading we find our "pearl of great price" and we move at once to think of ways to put it to use.

You can see how this kind of reading can be applied to any devotional literature. We focus it in Scripture, however, because this is the Book above all books. It is the Book of God which provides an essential objectivity to our spiritual formation, and a necessary basis for discrimination as we read and hear other ideas. Spiritual reading will take us into many books, but never away from the text or truth of God's Book.

† The next rung on our spiritual ladder is meditation. Prayer plays a vital role in spiritual formation. Through it we cultivate a sense of personal communion and communication with God. Remember, our working definition of spiritual formation is "friendship with God." Friends talk. They keep in touch.

They share their lives with each other. That's what prayer is. And it is an essential element in our formation.[7]

Meditation is a particular type of prayer—one which is misunderstood and misused in our time. For many, it conjures up notions of unbridled mysticism, exotic visions, and cultic experiences. We can almost see the meditator floating a few inches off the floor and mumbling his mantra. No wonder we shy away from it!

Meditation in non-Christian settings usually involves an attempt to empty the mind. Christian meditation is the process of filling the mind. Non-Christian meditation may well be related to a random stream-of-consciousness. Christian meditation is a focused reflection on a particular objective piece of material—a passage in the Bible, secondary devotional material, a hymn, or phrase from one of the historic creeds. Meditation is included as a type of prayer because it is a disposition of mind and heart which brings us into dialogue with God.

Well then, how do you meditate? You'll immediately see some connections with our previous description of spiritual reading. But let me add some additional features. After you select your material for meditation, the first step is to slowly and *carefully read every word.* If there are terms you do not understand, take time to look them up in a dictionary.

The second step is often *repetitive reading* of the material, putting the emphasis on different words to catch shades of meaning. If you're meditating on Scripture, this can include reading the verse from several translations. Repetition helps to implant the passage in your mind, and reveals how multifaceted the passage is when different parts of it are emphasized.

The third step is *selection,* as you focus on that part of the material which has most personally spoken to you. For example, in Philippians 1:5, Paul wrote of people who had been partners with him "from the first day until now." When I read those words, my mind fastened on them. I realized that I had people like that in my life—people who have supported me since I first became a Christian. I used the rest of my devotional time to name them, write their names in my journal, and give thanks for each one of them.

Selection can also include comparing the material you're meditating on with other material. For example, I never read John 1:14, "The Word became flesh and dwelt among us" without thinking of many ideas which E. Stanley Jones had concerning this passage. These words may lead me to think also of theological expressions on the theme of Incarnation. They may connect with a hymn like "Holy, Holy, Holy" where I'm reminded that God is "One in three Persons, blessed Trinity." These and other selections can enhance my meditation experience.

Finally, as with spiritual reading, meditation calls me to *accountability and action.* Meditation is always practiced for the purpose of amendment and improvement of life, and is fruitless if left suspended in space. We should come away from the experience, not with a blank mind, but with a renewed heart for God. We come out, not with glazed eyes, but with a clearer vision. And that's why the saints of the ages have included meditation as an essential ingredient in their spiritual formation.

† The next rung on the ladder is self-examination. Through spiritual reading and meditation, we receive significant impressions from God. Self-examination is the process of asking, "How does all this apply to me?" When we study the history of Christian spirituality, we find the discipline of self-examination to be something many of the saints practiced daily, usually toward evening. Some of them, like John Wesley and Jonathan Edwards, devised elaborate schemes and lists of questions to be used in their examinations. Whether elaborate or simple, the discipline is designed to bring one's life into submission to the truth.

Some people shy away from self-examination because it may lead them into negative thinking. When we lay our lives up against God's Word, we don't fare so well. But to avoid self-examination for that reason is to miss its point. A fever does not cease simply because we throw away the thermometer. Neither do our problems vanish because we stop paying attention to them. Self-examination, like the thermometer, is intended to give us a reading on the overall condition of our lives. It is not a condemnation or a judgment, but an evaluation to which we can then respond appropriately.

Self-examination must be balanced, particularly if we are prone to low self-esteem and negative thinking. We should not end our time of examination without allowing ourselves the gracious opportunity to celebrate successes and victories as well. By the same token, some of us who can rarely see our faults need to practice self-examination to find areas where change is needed. The key for both types of people is to keep it balanced, with appropriate attention to positive as well as negative areas. We can fall into a trap if we pay attention only to our failures. Balanced examination will save us from despair and depression. It will also save us from shallow, naive positivism.

† The processes of spiritual reading, meditation, and self-examination will inevitably lead us to the final discipline we want to consider—service. An outward expression of the spiritual life is essential. Otherwise, spiritual formation becomes another self-help program turned inward. We cannot practice spiritual reading, meditation, and self-examination without coming in touch with such ideas as involvement, mission, stewardship, neighborliness, morality, etc.

One of the ways we test our "heart for God" is in whether that heart is moving us beyond ourselves. It is the nature of God to extend Himself, and as He dwells within us, He creates that same desire. We are temples of the Holy Spirit, but that Spirit is never content to stay within the walls of the temple. Like the wind, He blows wherever He wills. And if our sails are up, we will move with Him.

This look at preparation is not intended to provide a comprehensive catalog of attitudes and actions related to spiritual formation. As you read further in the literature of Christian devotion, you will discover many other ideas and disciplines to enrich your formation. I have merely tried to provide elements related to preparation that focus on the individual. In the next chapter, I want us to examine those elements in our formation which bring us into contact with others. For while the journey of spiritual formation is personal, it is not solitary.

COUNTING THE COST

Suppose one of you wants to build a tower. Will he not first sit down and estimate the cost to see if he has enough money to finish it?   Luke 14:28

PRACTICE SILENCE

Think of the comprehensiveness of Christianity. Consider the tendency to reduce it or cheapen it.

PRACTICE REFLECTION

Plan one day that contains receiving, reflecting, recording, and responding. Focus specifically on the discipline of spiritual reading, particularly on John 1:1-18, using the four elements.

PRACTICE RESOLUTION

Determine to use a regular period of self-examination as a means of finding and maintaining a balanced perspective on your life.

PRACTICE PRAYER

Compose a prayer of praise and thanksgiving to God for making you the way you are. Then compose a prayer of confession and petition, asking God to be at work on your rough edges.

PRACTICE READING

Psalm 139:23-24 and 2 Corinthians 3:18

SEVEN

WE NEED EACH OTHER

As an ordained clergyman living in a seminary community, I conduct or attend quite a few weddings each year. As I have gone to more and more weddings, I have been increasingly impressed with the significance of names. In most cases, the bride takes the surname of the groom. In some cases, they join their surnames as a symbol of their new union. In all cases, the act of naming is one of the most meaningful parts of a marriage ceremony.

Every person born into the world is given a name. We do not understand human identity apart from names. The names we are given place us within a family, and throughout our lives, we exist in some sort of family context. Throughout our time on earth, we are people in community, and the family community exerts a powerful influence on our development.

This social reality is a reflection of a deeper, spiritual truth, one that is of utmost significance for spiritual formation. As Henri Nouwen put it, "The question is not simply, 'Where does God lead *me* as an individual person who tries to do His will?' More basic and more significant is the question, 'Where does God lead *us* as a people?' "[1] Spiritual formation recognizes and emphasizes that authentic spirituality exists only within the context of community. As individuals seeking to be more deeply formed by the Spirit, we realize that we need each other.

One of my greatest apprehensions regarding spiritual formation is that it will be considered an individualized, privatized, and largely hidden experience. So much of what we have been talking about can be *practiced* alone that it is very easy to be misled into thinking that spiritual formation and Christian maturation can be *achieved* alone. However, *nothing* which we've seen in previous chapters can be authentic apart from a commitment to life in community.

More than once during my pastoral ministry, I had people say something like, "I believe it is possible to be just as spiritual at home as it is at church." Or, "I can worship God just as truly in my garden as I can in the sanctuary." Of course, these comments were always used as a rationale for not attending public worship or for not becoming involved in the life of the church. Now, as I work in spiritual formation, I frequently hear the same kinds of remarks about personal devotion, solitude, retreat, etc. They contain truth to a certain extent, and they sound especially relevant in an individualistic generation. But all of them fall short of capturing the reality of the spiritual life.

One of the surest tests of the validity of our spiritual life is whether or not it produces within us the desire for community. Whenever the Spirit of God is at work in an individual, He will move that person toward others. The early monks who had lived as hermits discovered this. Under Benedict the monks were brought into communities called monasteries. If those who lived the most solitary spiritual lives recognized the need for community, we can do no less and still claim an authentic spirituality.

It is impossible to read the Bible without discovering community. Even in Creation, God acknowledged that it was not good for Adam to be alone. So Eve was created and families begun. At the time of the Flood, a family was salvaged and from them new families emerged. Later, God's covenant with Abraham was to make through him "a great nation." The rest of the Old Testament can be read as a story of that nation.

With the opening of the New Testament, the theme continues, as extended genealogies of Matthew and Luke tie the coming of the Messiah into the very fabric of the Jewish nation. Jesus was born into a family. He lived out His public ministry in a family setting with the disciples. At Pentecost, those disciples were even more closely linked through the birth of the church. And the rest of the New Testament is the story of the development and expansion of that church. Even the Book of Revelation shows us that life in community will continue forever in heaven.

Christians are truly "the family of God." To experience the life of God in our souls is to be drawn into a community. It is to be led from one community to another whenever we change locations. It is to pass from one community to another at the end of our life on earth—from the church visible to the church invisible. Spiritual formation cannot be genuine unless people catch this vision and experience this reality.

In this chapter, I want to make some general comments about the nature of our community life. And second, I will describe some basic models where this community can take place. I hope these considerations will help you appreciate the community you're in even more. Or, if you are not a part of a vital Christian fellowship, that you will be motivated to become part of one as an essential dimension of your spiritual growth.

THE NATURE OF COMMUNITY

We must begin by reminding ourselves that community is not something we can take for granted. Many of you will remember the Campus Crusade "I Found It" campaign of the seventies. This was an intensive, nationwide evangelistic effort aimed at bringing people into the Christian faith. There were media events, billboards, and even bumper stickers, all communicating the theme. More than a decade later, I still meet people who became Christians through that massive program.

However, even the leaders of the "I Found It" program admitted that their greatest problem was assimilating converts into local churches. Many more people reported individual conversion than were ever actually processed into the life of a congregation. A man who worked in the follow-up phase of the program in a large Southwestern city told me that time after time he would call one of the persons who had reported a conversion and tell them of a local church nearby where they could continue their faith development. Sometimes they would actually hang up before he could finish. And other times they would thank him for the information, but declare that they had no intention of becoming part of a Christian church.

After over thirty years of worldwide evangelistic crusades, Billy Graham still struggles with the problem of assimilating converts into local churches. Every parachurch organization I know of has a commitment to and structure for such assimilation. The problem lies more with the individuals than with the organizations. For all of us, it is too easy to stop with personal commitment. This is especially true in a time when many mainline denominations are bland in their common life and some independent churches are on the fringes of fanaticism. This encourages many people to opt for a personalized version of Christianity.

We must guard against the tendency toward isolation. Community is not optional. It is not like an accessory we buy for an automobile—nice, but not necessary. Community is part of being Christian. To be a follower of Christ the King is to be part of His kingdom. To be a member of the body of Christ is to express that commitment through some aspect of the Church. It pleases God to make spiritual realities tangible; the Church is a visible manifestation of God in the world. Those of us who walk with God will be committed to the church.

† Second, we should remember that community and compatibility are not synonymous. Henri Nouwen puts it well, "Community is grounded in God, who calls us together, and not in the attractiveness of people to each other."[2] Dietrich

Bonhoeffer, who studied Christian community as much as anyone ever has, recognized that mutual attraction and affection
cannot be the basis for genuine Christian community. He saw
that "community with one another consists solely in what Christ
has done for (all) of us."[3]

This is a much-needed word for Christians today. As I
travel around the country, I meet and hear about Christians who
are trying to form community on the basis of being with people
they like. Often, we appoint and call pastors on the basis of how
much we like them. We start Sunday School classes with people
who like each other. People will change churches and even
denominations using the rationale, "We like this one better." And
while I am not against finding community and fellowship with
people we like, I recognize that this cannot be the *basis* for
Christian community.

The basis for community is the fact that you and I are
followers of the same Lord. If in the providence of God we are
brought together, then we must accept that and allow the Spirit
to create community between us. This community may be ce-
mented partly by our affinity and affection, but it will not stop
there. Community exists even in the midst of difference, and
sometimes even confrontation. Community is not a guarantee of
continual happiness and ease.

We can take a lesson from human family life. We did not
choose our families. And most of us can fantasize a more perfect
family than we have. Community in a family setting has little to
do with mutual compatibility. In fact, there are ages and stages
when we find compatibility to be a rare and precious commodity.
Community in the family is sustained by commitment day by day
that works through the differences and continues through the
struggles. This is why the Christian marriage ceremony is based
on vows of commitment rather than on feelings of ecstasy.

Any community formed on the basis of like-mindedness,
mutual affection, doctrinal sameness, or even felt need, is bound

to disintegrate sooner or later. Compatibility is a poor foundation for authentic Christian community. The grace of God operating in and through people is the basis of the church. Any two genuine Christians should be able to study, worship, pray, serve, or play together. The extent to which we are unable to do so is the extent we have yet to learn about community.

    † Third, authentic communities are by no means places where stress and tension are absent. In fact, you can guarantee "growing pains" wherever Christians are attempting to develop genuine community. Sister Miriam Murphy, a contemporary writer on the life of prayer, lists the following as some natural tensions that create problems in communities: commitment to committees, slavery to procedure, group pressure, naivete, and the natural processes of group dynamics. [4] For her, only agape love can cement people in community.

    In the course of my ministry, God has permitted me to work with people who were about to drop out of mainline churches and join or start independent ones. One of the things I've noticed is that people tend to leave where they do not feel loved or where they feel unable to express love to others in the fellowship. This is tragic enough, but there is something else here that is also damaging. People who leave because they cannot express love often find it hard to love the new group. In other words, this lack of love which caused them to leave in the first place may be repeated in the new location, much to their surprise, since they thought they were headed toward the "promised land." When a breakdown of love is the problem, change of location or people is not the answer.

    What does this mean for community? It means that tension and difficulty should not throw us. These are not the things which destroy community. In fact, when handled and managed wisely, they can even strengthen it. No, what destroys community is the deterioration of love. For when we cannot love one another, we cannot find much else that will hold us together. This means that as we build community, we must never stop growing in love for each other. Otherwise, the natural problems and tensions of group life will become avenues of decay and maybe even death.

† Fourth, community is expressed in degrees. Thomas Kelly wrote that no one person "can hold *all* dedicated souls within his compass in steadfast fellowship with equal vividness."[5] Within every community there will be relationships of varying intensity, depth, and regularity. This is a sign of healthy group life and it should not become a source of jealousy or competition.

This needs to be mentioned because the idea persists that Christian community should reflect equality in relationships. Leaders especially are vulnerable to the criticism of "playing favorites" or "forming cliques." To be sure, this is a danger in community which must be carefully monitored and studiously avoided. But at the same time, members in the community must not fall prey to the false assumption that leaders can relate to everyone exactly alike or that members can know each other equally well.

Instead, as we enter into community we should seek those few, special relationships which are waiting for us as gifts of God. There will come times when these special friends will be channels of His grace. Right now, I hope you can name several such people in your community of faith. And I trust that you are functioning this way for some people in the group. It's a natural and necessary part of Christian community.

Moving out from these few, you will discover other important but less meaningful relationships. Such people can provide stimulation, support, and enjoyment—all necessary ingredients in community. And then finally, there will be those people whom you only know by sight. But even they will be important, for they will be additional reminders of the reality of Christianity and the fact that there are many on a journey similar to yours.

† This idea connects with the fact that community is not determined by frequency of contact between given individuals. Frequency is desirable but not essential. Again Thomas Kelly provides perspective, "Weeks and months and even years may elapse, yet the reality remains undimmed."[6] This idea must not be misinterpreted to mean that regular contact plays a minor role in the formation of community. But it is an important reminder that the genius of community is not in being "together" at every opportunity.

I watch community-building efforts at the seminary. One of the first questions asked is, "How often should we meet?" The assumption underneath the question is that the more often we meet, the better the community will be. Frequency may be more of a need in the beginning of a community, but it must not be allowed to be the controlling principle as the group develops and matures.

When Jeannie and I were in seminary, we formed a meaningful group relationship with three other couples. To this day, these people remain significant friends, even though we are all hundreds of miles from each other. But we nearly killed the relationship by mistakenly assuming that we had to be together as often as possible. This included a weekly group meeting that usually lasted several hours and expanded to include other social contacts during the week. We became consumed by each other. Our relational world shrunk and our sense of community became myopic. Without knowing it, we were smothering each other. Thank God, we finally realized this and pulled back in time to save the community and our friendship.

When community is characterized by lengthy passages of time between meetings, there is some loss of intimacy and a resulting sadness. But community itself is not destroyed. One of the couples in that group remain our dearest friends on earth, even though we rarely see them. The depth and reality of our community is felt when we do get together. It is as if we have never been apart. Oh sure, we've lost touch on many things and we've a lot of catching up to do. But the relationship is there! And that's an important test and proof for genuine community, especially among those closest to us.

Marriage literature stresses the need for couples to give each other space. People need times of closeness and intimacy. But they also require time to be alone, time to cultivate personal interests, time to be themselves without living under the shadow of another's influence. The same is true in the formation of Christian community. Dietrich Bonhoeffer describes this in his classic work, *Life Together*, as he shows how community is structured around the rhythm of being together and being apart. He makes the powerful point that community must never become a substitute for solitude. "Many people seek fellowship because they are afraid to be alone. Because they cannot stand loneliness, they are driven to seek the company of other people."[7]

Community is not given to us by God as an escape from living with ourselves. The group is not a place where we can become absorbed in a corporate identity so we do not have to face our individuality. Just the opposite is true—we will find community richer to the extent that we can enter it and then leave it. To demand it or to cling to it is to destroy it.

† Sixth, community is nourished in a sacramental fellowship. This means that true spirituality is always expressed in relation to the church. It also means that the focus of community is not the group, but God. And it means that the life of the group does not come by creativity or sound dynamics, but by the grace of God. Grace is the invisible factor which gives the group its soul. Perhaps you have been in a group that had all the right mechanics but lacked vitality. Similarly, you may have been in a group that had some functional weaknesses, but still was vibrant. The grace of God is the difference.

In spiritual formation this sacramental dimension is

essential, if spirituality is to be saved from the privatistic experience we talked about earlier.[8] By definition, the sacraments of the church are practiced in community. They should not be administered by unauthorized individuals, because they belong to the body. This fact alone makes them important in relationship to community life. This is seen in several significant ways.

Through baptism we find our initiation point into the family of God. It is here that the church and the baptized person witness to the fact that God's grace has a claim on every human life. The focal point of that grace is the Cross, where God claimed us centuries before any of us were even born. Our faith response to that grace at our baptism indicates that we consciously choose to be followers of Christ's Way and to identify ourselves with His community. For those of us who are already members, baptism is the sacred act of receiving new people into the fellowship and celebrating that God's grace continues to claim and call people.

Having entered into this fellowship, we find the sacrament of the Lord's Supper to be especially meaningful. As we partake of Communion, our sense of community is nourished in several important ways.

First, we are participating with the church universal. Christians in every century have participated in this sacrament. Communion is the most tangible expression of our connectedness as Christians. It binds us to every other Christian on earth, and also to the saints in heaven. We are never closer to one another than when we partake of the Lord's Supper.

Second, we kneel together as an act of recognition that Jesus is truly present to meet our needs individually and to strengthen our fellowship collectively. Christians have differed as to *how* Christ is present at Communion, but we all believe He is there in some way. Communion is no barren ritual, but is a drawing near to Christ Himself through the service He Himself instituted. He chooses to meet us at Communion and to feed our souls according to their need.

And third, we experience Communion as a foretaste of glory—a glory that will be perfect, unbroken, and eternal in heaven. Our reception of the Lord's Supper is a reminder that the community which is formed on earth will never end. The reception of the elements is but a foretaste of the heavenly banquet where all the saints of God feast in perfect and unbroken fellowship. Our unity at the table on earth is a foreshadowing of the heavenly unity which far exceeds anything we have known here on earth. Our communion here is an important preparation for what we will do there.

All of this takes place in the context of worship, which is a primary means of spiritual formation. Dr. Donald Saliers describes the relationship between spiritual formation and worship by saying that the primary value of worship is that it regularly calls us to remembrance.[9] Through prayers, hymns, sermons, and sacraments we are called to remember the heritage which is ours, the faith which we have experienced, the fellowship which binds us together, and the aims and purposes to which we are committed as believers.

And with respect to community, forgetfulness is one of the primary eroding factors. We forget what brought us together in the first place. We forget our dependency on the grace of God. We forget how precious we are to the Lord, and how special we should be to each other. We forget what we exist for. And it goes on and on. Worship, as an act of remembrance, is of utmost importance to the maintenance of community. We need this kind of sacramental fellowship, not only for our individual soul's health, but also for the development of healthy and growing corporate relationships.

† This leads to a seventh and final comment about community. Its goal is greater obedience.[10] Everything else is secondary, though not unimportant. We need each other because through fellowship we are enabled to live out our faith

with greater vitality and consistency. Community provides these essential ingredients out of which obedience comes and flourishes: unity, accountability, encouragement, correction, instruction, and support.

When Jesus sent out the disciples, He sent them in groups of two. There is strength in numbers—people can pick each other up, they can put salve on wounds, they can provide laughter and fun. They can say, "Hang in there!" when we are tempted to give up and turn back. I have often said that because of community I have a stronger faith than I would have if I were alone. For through the experience and witness of others, I discover aspects of God and Christianity which have not been part of my own experience. Through community I am spurred on to be a more obedient follower of Jesus.

MODELS OF COMMUNITY

There's so much more that could be said about the value of community. My purpose has not been to be exhaustive, but rather motivating. I hope I've said enough for you to be convinced that community is an indispensable element in spiritual formation. If I have, then the next question inevitably is, "How can I participate in this kind of community?" For the rest of the chapter, I want to provide a very basic look at where community is to be discovered and enjoyed.

† I believe the primary place where it occurs is in the family. I began this chapter by looking at a wedding ceremony, for the wedding serves as the launching pad for a brand new family. And it represents the joining of two previous families in the new unit thus created. In the economy of God, the family becomes the foundational formative unit on earth.

Unfortunately, this unit is under siege in our society. It is estimated that by 1990, one-half of the children in America will live some of their years in single-parent homes. And in many more homes which look traditional, one or both of the parents will have been divorced and remarried. It is a phenomenon which sociologists say will have a profound effect on society. It will necessarily also have an effect on the spirituality of our people.

Those of us who are fortunate to still be part of a healthy, traditional family setting must not take this for granted. And even if you are reading this as a single parent or as one who has remarried, never underestimate the influence of your family. Through your loved ones, God is working to communicate essential personal and social factors which will affect you for the rest of your life.

In Christian circles, we frequently hear spiritual formation discussed in relation to family devotions. I want to go on record as recognizing the importance of family worship." But I also want to paint a larger picture of family formation than just the minutes we spend in family devotions. The community significance of the family cannot be limited to the time a family spends together in devotion, for it is much broader than that.

While this is not a book devoted to spiritual formation in the family, I cannot in good conscience fail to list some of the more important elements related to family:

1. The family provides the arena for caring and nurturing.
2. It teaches the necessity and blessedness of giving.
3. It creates a worldview and a vision for what life can be.
4. It helps its members develop resiliency and flexibility.
5. It facilitates the experience of parental "letting go."
6. It creates a healthy sense of dependency and appreciation for others.
7. It teaches us to recognize and appreciate the value of routine and ordinary life.

8. It gives us a sense of connection with the past and the future.
9. It allows the space for individuality to grow and mature.
10. It trains us to learn to live with life as it is, while holding motivation to improve it.
11. It gives us ample opportunity to practice the art of forgiveness.
12. It teaches how to play, and to appreciate the value of play.
13. It teaches the qualities of humility, acceptance, service, etc.
14. It offers essential direction in matters of morality, religion, and values.
15. It provides a living model for children of what marriage is.
16. It leads us to discover God and commit ourselves to Him. [12]

Little wonder then that we cannot contain all of this under the heading of family devotions, although much of it can at least be communicated and discussed through the medium of family worship. More important is the daily, ongoing modeling of these concepts. This kind of life is caught as much as it is taught. And because these qualities are so essential to healthy development, God entrusts their communication in the most intimate of communities, the family.

I realize that some of you who are reading this will not be able to identify with all that I have said. Your own experience of family life did not provide positive and healthy examples of this kind of living. I see this more and more, even among men and women who are in seminary preparing to be leaders in the church. There is much relearning that has to take place, even in the Christian fellowship. Let me say two things to those of you who do not come out of a family unit that provided you with this kind of experience.

First, the church is the family of God. Many of the qualities mentioned above can be found in a congregation of believers who love Jesus. Find a church like that and sink your roots into the soil of its life. You will be nourished by that family. Not long ago two sisters joined our church. I noticed that their parents were not present, and I found out that they came from a home that was far from the standards of Christianity. But these sisters, both in their teens, had Christian friends. They came to see that in the church they could find many of the things their own family had failed to provide. You can do the same even if your own family does not offer a Christian way of life.

The second thing to say is that community life and formation is not limited to the family context. There are many expressions of community which are desirable for all of us. In one way or another, we should all be seeking to incorporate these expressions of community into our spiritual formation.

† I begin with the need for us to have a few close *friends*. In chapter 3 we spoke about the ministry of spiritual friendship or spiritual direction. I am not referring to that here. Rather, I am talking about the natural and necessary network of friendly relationships. Each of us needs to have a few close friends with whom we can share life. This broad foundation of sharing creates the atmosphere for more specific and personal communication when the occasion calls for it.

I have several such persons in my life and I thank God for each of them. Much of the time we go through the motions of general friendship. But because we have committed ourselves to each other in that way, we are able to move to deeper issues when the situation calls for it. Basil Pennington has captured the importance of this friendship in these words, "Anyone who has been graced by true friendship knows the cost and knows the worth."[13]

This kind of friendship has been modeled for us in the

Moravian and Wesleyan traditions through what were called Bands. Bands were groups of from three to five persons who related to each other regularly and deeply. The Bands were made up of people of the same sex because it was felt there were some things which men needed to share with men, and things women needed to share with women. They functioned primarily for encouragement and support, and were places where honest confession could be made without fear of rejection. The bonds of friendship which united these people were strong enough to hold under any circumstances.

I hope you have a friend, or several friends to whom you can relate at this level. They are a necessary part of Christian community. The meetings can be scheduled, or they can simply flow out of the normal interaction that you have as friends. You will have to decide the structure which best facilitates the relationship. The element to capture is that of deep communion in the larger context of normal friendship.

Before we leave this level, there are a couple of practical matters which often come up when this kind of relationship is discussed. The first has to do with whether your spouse can or should be included at this level of spiritual community. I answer in two ways. First, your spouse should provide for even more intimate sharing than can be found in a small friendship group. I believe that a spouse is given to us by God to be *the* closest person on earth. The only deeper level of relationship is in that "holy of holies" when we commune alone with God at the deepest and most private level. So I include our spouses at this level.

At the same time, I stress the need for a friendship group that does not include spouses. We need a few people beyond our spouse with whom we can share at virtually the same level. In fact, there will be a few occasions when the group will receive and process things from you which you would not want to share with your spouse. In community, we do not need to be limited to our spouse for deep sharing.

A second issue has to do with whether it is preferable to have this Band-group relationship to include people of the opposite sex. I've probably already given the answer in the description above. At this level, I do not believe it is best. I think it is preferable to have men sharing with men and women with women. Recent studies on bonding have shown that there is a close connection between spirituality and sexuality, and I believe it can be risky to regularly and deeply bare our souls before a person of the opposite sex who is not our spouse.[14] I do not rule out the need for spiritual relationships with persons of the opposite sex. I simply believe that they should occur at another level.

† The next level of community is that of a meaningful group or two. Here I'm thinking of a larger fellowship group of perhaps eight to ten, the typical small group that we hear about today.[15] Oftentimes, these will be made up of people who know each other fairly well. And it is in this context that meaningful sharing with persons of the opposite sex can take place.

Since group members should have the network of close friendships to draw on, the tone of the larger group should not be confessional. Rather, it should be a place to celebrate, support, study, and encourage one another. Issues relating to vocation and parenting can be meaningfully shared in such groups, but the focus will not be on the sharing of the deeper issues which the smaller friendship group can provide.

I believe one of the primary functions of this larger group should be prayer. This can occur through hymn and chorus singing, in a reflective study of Scripture and contemporary literature, and as we enter into intercessory prayer for group members and people outside. The atmosphere of the group should be such that we sense we have met God together.

Unless your group is exceptional, I think it is best not to form it on a "till death us do part" basis. There should be fixed points of beginning and ending. People should have a chance to buy into and out of the group relationship as circumstances of their lives dictate. This does not mean that participation is haphazard or shallow—people should be faithful for the time which they have committed to be together. But it does mean that they can move in and out of the group without feeling pressure or guilt. Each new beginning can be a time for some to leave and others to join. This will provide a sense of liberty and realism, no one is "locked in" to the relationship.

Groups of this nature will grow along paths of common interest and need. They will have the joy of watching each other mature in the faith. They will feel a bond of strength and support which is necessary to support meaningful spiritual development. They will experience the necessity and value of corporate wisdom and insight. And they will learn to appreciate the differences that men and women bring to the topics which are explored by the group. All of these are healthy benefits to our spiritual development.

There is a problem to be noted, however. Occasionally, people are involved in too many groups, and this can be counterproductive to spiritual formation. For one thing, it divides their attention to multiple agendas. And it can easily overload them, especially if each group is committed to study between sessions. I would recommend that you limit yourself to one or two groups. For example, you might be part of a weekly men's or women's fellowship and a member of a group with your spouse. Remember, your spirituality is not a matter of quantity, but quality. Use this as the test of your community experiences.

† A fourth level of community occurs in the church. This is the core group for Christian community, although it may not be the group in which you do your most meaningful interacting. This is especially true if you worship in a large congregation. I call the church the core group because no other group should become a substitute for regular and committed participation in it.

There is something wrong if other levels of community become alternatives for the church.

Here is where the witness of church history can help us. There have always been subcommunities in the Christian Church. The Protestant Reformers especially recognized the validity of and need for "little churches" within the larger church. Their function was to provide meaningful fellowship and to maintain community between the worship services of the church.

The experience of early Methodism is a good example of this principle. As John Wesley formed the United Societies in England, he forbade these groups from meeting at the same time that worship services were being held in the Church of England. Furthermore, anyone who became a member of the United Societies was expected and encouraged to maintain full participation in a church. Wesley's hope was that the formation of community in the "little church" would produce people who would enrich the life of the larger Church.

Spiritual formation seeks to produce people who are loyal to their church. This includes faithful participation in a Sunday School class. It means worshiping regularly. And it means serving in positions of responsibility and leadership. Those who are being properly formed will be conscientious in their affiliation with the church.

† This leads to a final level of community in spiritual formation. We will seek to find some expressions of community in the world. In the next chapter I want to develop this idea more fully, for a danger in spiritual formation is to become so preoccupied with our growth that we neglect service in the world. True spirituality continues to seek presence and influence in the world.

It is a tragedy when Christians believe that they cannot associate with people who are not Christian. To be sure, we must not continue relationships that destroy the very faith and life we profess. But neither must we fall prey to the notion that Christians should only associate and socialize with Christians. This attitude not only contradicts the very example which Christ gave, but it also reveals a bad theology and a faulty spirituality.

As a bad theology, it says that Christians had better not associate with non-Christians because the non-Christians might "contaminate" the Christians. Whatever happened to our belief that "greater is He that is in you than he that is in the world"? Friendship with non-Christians should not blind us to the lure of temptation, nor make us indiscriminate in our relationships. But it should remind us that if we are truly guided by the Spirit, we have the armor of God to protect us as we live and interact in the world.

Furthermore, it's a bad theology because it cuts the nerve of evangelism. When I was in seminary in the early 1970s, I heard D. James Kennedy say that our problem was that we had ceased to be fishers of men and had become keepers of the aquarium. When Christians cease meaningful relations with non-Christians, they cease having an evangelistic presence. I find no evidence from the Book of Acts or the Letters of Paul that the Christians retreated from the world. Rather, I find them seeking ways to increase their contact with non-Christians.

It is a faulty spirituality if we turn in on ourselves and become conspicuous consumers of the spiritual life. It is a faulty spirituality which severs contact with neighbors and associates who do not know God as we do. It is a faulty spirituality which narrows our experience of life to only those things clearly labeled as "Christian." Our purpose is not to create lists of Christian associations, Christian music, Christian books, Christian businesses, and Christian places. Our challenge is to live in the world without becoming seduced by it. Our goal is to relate to non-Christians without losing our convictions. Our responsibility is to penetrate a secularized society with values that can improve it. True spiritual formation will equip and strengthen us for living in the world as we find it.

When I was a child, the Colgate-Palmolive Company ran commercials on TV about the "invisible shield" which its toothpaste was supposed to put on our teeth to fight cavities. Spiritual formation is not an invisible shield that separates us from people, or makes us self-sufficient, self-generating people. Our life in Christ is always nourished by outside sources—the Spirit of God and our association with others. Christian community on a variety of levels nourishes our spirituality and provides avenues to express it. We are the richer precisely because we need each other.

EXPERIENCING COMMUNITY

Let us consider how we may spur one another on toward love and good deeds. Let us not give up meeting together, as some are in the habit of doing, but let us encourage one another—and all the more as you see the Day approaching. Hebrews 10:24-25

PRACTICE SILENCE

Think about dimensions of Christianity you share in community. How are you dependent on others for your development?

PRACTICE REFLECTION

Evaluate the quality of your community life in relation to spouse, family, friends, group, church, and society. List positives and negatives.

PRACTICE RESOLUTION

Determine by God's grace to fulfill one specific action in each of the above areas during the next three months.

PRACTICE PRAYER

Name before God the most significant persons in your life. Give thanks to God for each of them.

PRACTICE READING

Psalm 122 and Philippians 1:3-11

EIGHT

INTO THE WORLD

Karl Marx declared religion to be the opiate of the people. Ironically, it can be. Anytime religion becomes so personal and privatized that it dulls our sense of servanthood in the world, it has drugged us. Unfortunately, history records examples of religion doing this very thing. Stories still come out of the South documenting how the church sought to legitimize slavery. And now and then we hear reports from World War II Germany of how the church remained silent in the face of the Jewish holocaust. Such gross perversions of faith are easy to identify.

However, even something good like spiritual formation can be diverted into selfishness and away from servanthood. Left unchecked, the quest for spiritual maturation can turn into another self-improvement program with a thin veil of religiosity over it. If we are to avoid this pitfall, we must see our spiritual development in the context of a needy world, and realize that our life in Christ calls us to be involved in that world.

If spiritual formation becomes another I-Me experience, it will—and should—fall by the wayside. However, if we can harness personal growth to social responsibility, then we have the potential for making an impact on our generation.

NO MERE MORTALS

For millions of people today, life is defined in terms of self-centeredness and personal acquisition. One of the most graphic examples of that is a television commercial which declares, "You only go around once in life, so you've got to grab all the gusto you can."

That's it—the core issue is that each of us has a choice. We can become grabbers or givers. The call to become other-oriented is at the heart of Christianity. But response to that call means swimming against the current.

For one thing, we go against the current of ego. Theologians have argued, and continue to argue, about the nature and expression of original sin. I believe it can be essentially described as egocentrism. The fact that we have egos is not a sign of original sin. Our unique "self" is part of the original plan of God for humanity. The problem is when "self" becomes our god and we worship it. We try to make all of life revolve around it. We seek to gratify it. And this "self" comes to occupy a place of centrality which it was never intended to have. It happened in the Garden, and it continues to happen today.

The current phenomenon of Yuppyism represents a view of life which is selfish at its core. Studies of today's upwardly mobile young people show them to be less concerned about servanthood than their counterparts of even a decade ago. Part of this is due to the belief that the world's problems are simply too big to be solved. So in exchange for a missional perspective on life, they take revised versions of "eat, drink, and be merry, for tomorrow we die."

For another thing, this other-orientation swims against the current of our senses. Our deep-seated egocentricity is fed by the senses. Most advertising in our society focuses on gratification of the senses. Commercials do not ask us to think; they ask us to feel, to want, to desire. Much of industry is based more on how to get things done for the cheapest price, than for the concern of workers. In political circles, national self-interest often rules in the determination of policy. On a more personal level, almost from the time we wake up in the morning until we go to bed at night, we are in a sea of sensuality which fuels our selfishness.

So, it is not easy to have an other-orientation in life. And there are no surefire, no-fail programs which can make it happen. One of our greatest challenges as Christians looking to the future is to communicate values and ethics which run counter to prevailing customs. The church not only faces a mammoth evangelistic task, but an equally demanding task of discipling those who accept Christ. Many Christians need help in understanding the distinctiveness of Christian values in the various areas of their lives.

Are we left at the mercy of our time? Or is there something we can do to begin to take on this new understanding of life? I believe there is a place to begin, but even here it is a place that requires conscious attention; it will not happen automatically. It is cultivating a vision of others which reflects the truth of C. S. Lewis' comment, "There are no ordinary people. You have never talked to a mortal."¹ It is training ourselves to remember that every person we meet is made in the image of God, just a little lower than the angels.

As a Christian in the Wesleyan tradition, I am informed and influenced by Wesley's emphasis on prevenient grace. This is the dimension of God's grace which is given to every person born into the world. It is the dimension of grace which prevents the Fall from totally dehumanizing us. It is the dimension of grace which continues to make us people of eternal value and objects of God's love, even after the entrance of sin. Two of Wesley's cardinal verses in this regard were these, "Through [the Word] all things were made; without Him nothing was made that has been made. . . . The true light that gives light to every man was coming into the world" (John 1:3, 9) and, "But God demonstrates His own love toward us, in that while we were still sinners, Christ died for us" (Romans 5:8).

The sadness is that many people in the world are either

unaware of this great truth, or refuse to live in harmony with it. Yet, this does not diminish God's love for them and it should not reduce our regard for them. We must never forget that we share some aspect of community with every other human being. Through a common creation we share the *imago dei* with every person we meet, and they with us. The possibility of redemption exists for every person. No one is beyond the reach of grace. No one is soulless.

Every time we depersonalize and dehumanize others by forgetting the sacredness of their humanity, we cut the nerve of other-orientedness. I remember during the Vietnam War the evening news gave almost daily reports concerning casualties. When our losses were cited, they were generally accompanied with one or two personal stories of soldiers and their families. But when the Vietcong's casualties were noted, they were simply referred to as "enemy losses." By keeping them nameless and faceless, their losses hit with much less emotional impact and seemed more justified. But every one of them had families who grieved too.

To lose this sense of creational community is to risk thinking of and relating to people as stereotypes. Here are some examples I still hear: All Jews are stingy. Catholics are not Christians. Northerners are not friendly. All Texans are braggarts. All Russians are Communists. America is a Christian nation.

If we live within the insulation of generalities, we are in danger of forgetting the preciousness of people. Christian spiritual formation never lets me forget that all people are made in the image of God, and as such, each person is unique and valuable.

I have to confess that I do not always think and react this way. I have to keep pulling myself up to this vision. One way I do it is by watching people in a public place like a mall or airport. I try to note something unique about each one of them, something that makes them different from anyone else in the crowd. Then I look for qualities or actions that remind me of God, even seemingly little things. A young man holds a door open for a handicapped person, and I think of God's patience with my limitations. A big brother holds the soft drink of his little sister while she ties her shoes, and I think how many things God holds for me. A hassled mother tries to shop with a crying baby in a stroller and a three-year-old tugging at her dress, and I remember how hard it is to be self-controlled. Two old people sit silently eating pie and coffee just looking at each other after all the years, and I remember God's never-ending love for me.

Some might say that I am involved in an exercise in spiritual sentimentalism. But in reality, I believe I am taking the opportunity to observe countless little expressions of our *imago dei* manifesting itself in daily life. I believe I am being gently reminded that every person is precious. The children's song is true, "Red and yellow, black and white, we are precious in His sight!"

If we can establish a vision of the sacredness of every person, then we will sense a call to become involved with them in their need. Our spirituality will be such that we *cannot* keep it to ourselves. We will ask God to make of us what St. Francis of Assisi prayed for, "Lord, make me an instrument of Thy peace." Our faith will be not only a gift to treasure, but also a blessing to share.

Frank Laubach, one of God's great servants of a past generation, used to begin his day by praying, "Lord, what are You doing in the world today that I can help You with?" E. Stanley Jones used to call his morning prayers the time when he got his "marching orders for the day." These attitudes capture the spirit we're describing here. They speak of a realization that we have awakened to a new day in order that Christ can minister through us to others.

Thomas Langford has suggested a practical way of putting this aspect of spirituality into practice. He says that we should take a "word for the day" during our morning prayers.[2] For example, we might take the word *patience*. Then as we move through the day, we can recall the word and see if we are exhibiting that quality in our relationships with others. As this becomes second nature to us, we will find that Christ is able to express more and more of His qualities to others through our attitudes and actions.

Would you agree with me today that we need a new understanding of life? I know I do. Even with these ideas in mind, I find too many of my days are more a reflection of a self-centered culture than of the purposes of God for His people. I have to keep calling myself back to this kind of spiritual vision. As I do, Henri Nouwen's words become increasingly true for me, "The mystery of ministry is that the Lord is to be found where we minister. . . . The more we give, help, support, guide, counsel, and visit, the more we receive, not just similar gifts, but the Lord Himself."[3]

PACING OURSELVES

A spirituality which takes us into the world leads us to a new understanding of pace. One of the reasons we do not find motivation for ministry in the world is that we are already too busy attending to our own lives. Busyness is a contemporary curse that afflicts us from childhood to the end of life. As I watch my own children caught up in it, I realize our society is doing an excellent job in producing tomorrow's workaholics.

In a technological age, we can get more done. Or at least we're told we can. Quantitatively we turn out impressive amounts of work. Life moves fast, seeming little more than a blur at times. We fall into bed at the end of the day and wonder what we really did. Our energies are soon drained and we have little left over for family, much less for the community and the world. Our homes become little caves into which we retreat. Neighbors are strangers, and the other side of town may as well not exist—much less the other side of the world.

The ultimate irony of a so-called leisure society is that we are busier than ever! Our lives are filled to the brim. Almost instinctively we draw back from calls to become involved in humanitarian activities, especially if the involvement means additional time and personal action. And so, from the perspective of spiritual formation, it must be said that this kind of pace is counterproductive. It is not the way God intended for us to live.

Constant activity can be addictive, so that we actually get hooked on it. Check yourself. What do you do when you have some spare moments? Do you know how to relax? Do you know how to use those moments for activities that are different in quality, not just quantity? Henri Nouwen has noted that boredom is one of the characteristics of our society.[4] Boredom is not so much an expression of fatigue as it is a statement that we have run out of things to do, or that what we're doing is no longer satisfying. Either way, it describes a quality of spirit that erodes our sense of missional living.

Studies of depression show that one of its causes is the consuming of too much time and energy on ourselves. The depressed person is often one who has put himself or herself at the center. The cure lies in helping the person to become other-oriented. Depression is often lifted when people begin to get involved in the lives of others. For many of us that requires a new sense of pace. We face schedules that simply do not allow time for servanthood. In order to find time to minister to others, we will have to drop some of our activities.

The corporate sector is increasingly seeing the wisdom of this kind of living. Many organizations encourage their employees to devote a certain amount of time to charitable and community service. A national newsmagazine reported that more people are seeking jobs which provide psychic as well as monetary income.[5] Psychic income includes a flexibility of time so that people can devote themselves to personally meaningful activities. By capitalizing on a spiritual principle, the business world is getting better work out of their employees.

A new understanding of pace will help us to purchase quality time to become involved in the world and its needs. We will not have to do it on the leftovers and with a begrudging spirit. A reordering of our lives will create some space which we can use to improve the world around us. But for those of us who are caught up in an activist, production-oriented lifestyle, such change will not be easy.

A number of years ago, I was wrestling with this as it pertained to my son. John and some of his friends were wanting to become Cub Scouts, but all the existing dens were full. The pack leader told me that it would be great for the boys to be in Cub Scouts, if a leader could be found to start a new den. Right then, the Spirit spoke to me, "You do it." But I tried to argue my way out of it—"Lord, You know I don't have time for this." But the Spirit persisted, "Then make time." And at that point, I realized that the pace at which I was living professionally had to be pared back to allow time to be a den leader.

I'd like to be able to tell you that I consistently reorder my life along these lines, but just like you, I struggle with busyness. However, experiences like my year as a den leader have convinced me that life's value consists in many things that don't appear on a job description. My spiritual formation includes the continual wrestling with pace, and the accompanying need to reorder my life.

MISSION

A third major movement toward the world is a new understanding of mission. One of our problems is that we put mission at too great a distance, when actually it is near at hand. The old hymn has reflected mission in the true sense, but we can too easily sing over the words which should guide us, "Though it be little, a neighborly deed—help somebody today."

Satan can cut the jugular vein of mission by telling us that we're not doing it because we have not surrendered at an altar for missionary service. As long as he can get us to professionalize missions, he will keep us from it. Jesus provided the true definition of mission when He told us that even a cup of cold water given in His name was not to be despised (Mark 9:41).

When I look at life through that lens, I see how much of my life is missional in nature. If I have an orientation toward others, and if I have paced myself so as to have time to really see people and their needs, then each day is filled with opportunities for ministry. It can come as I walk to and from classes. It may occur at the water fountain or during a break. It may take place out in the parking lot. It is practiced over the fence. There are opportunities for missional living where I am every day.

† For this to occur, however, I believe three qualities are necessary. And each quality is enhanced through the cultivation of our spiritual lives. The first I call insight. This means we must have some idea about where we are to minister for the good of others. This is where contemplation is valuable, for the contemplative life scans the horizon seeking for places and people in need of Christ. Even a few minutes of contemplation along this line yields a list of needs and names.

† Insight leads to focus. In our contemplating, we can easily feel overwhelmed by the sheer number of needs, much less their depth. This is a dangerous stage in missional living, for the seeds of inactivity can sprout when we see the immensity of need. This is why I constantly remind myself of the words of Thomas Kelly, "The Loving Presence does not burden us equally with all things, but considerately puts upon each of us just a few central tasks."[6]

Does this mean that we are free in Christ to be selective? I believe it does. But it is a selectivity which is done in faith, believing that as God leads us to select certain places and people, He is doing the same with others. And in this way all the bases can be covered. The debilitating fallacy is to think we're supposed to cover them all, and wear out trying to do it.

Here I am not talking about general and continual acts of kindness through the day, but rather of the special dimensions of missional ministry that we will give ourselves to. And the beauty of it is that the Lord is gracious and good to lay at our feet several such ministries. Sometimes they come to the surface after months of feeling drawn to them. Sometimes they come unexpectedly. But they come.

Recently and unexpectedly God has called me to a minor role in a ministry to burned-out, depleted clergy. At the moment, the involvement is limited. But as the ministry grows, my involvement may have to grow as well. The point is that the Lord laid this ministry at my feet and I felt it was one of the outreaches I was called to have at this time in my life. I am committed to it, and will have to adjust my involvement according to its demands.

† Determination of focus leads to action. Sooner or later, we must go to work. But right here I find that Christians are frequently confused and even bewildered. They can see a lot to do right in their own neighborhood. The local church annually lays before them certain priorities. Their mailboxes are filled with requests from a wide variety of organizations.

I offer the following only as counsel and as an example of how I've worked through the dilemma of knowing how and where to become involved. I believe there are three levels of involvement which are minimal if we are to have a world ministry. The first comes through the *local church* with which we have chosen to identify. This is the primary mission field of our activity. Making one's gifts and resources available for the edification of the body is something every Christian should do. I've been in churches large and small, and I have yet to find one that had all the help it needed.

The second level comes through *personal involvement in a cause* close to home, or at least close enough to have a hands-on relationship with it. Organizations need funds, but they also need people. We need to give ourselves to a cause that we believe in. I know a person who has found such a ministry through making tapes for the blind. This ministry is the result of her contemplation, which has now led to action. She receives great joy through it, and makes a valuable contribution to university students who need the tapes to further their education.

Another family I know of devotes one Saturday a month to work in our city's Community Kitchen. They not only provide a much-needed service, but they also have the joy of sharing in a ministry together. We can easily find such ministries; their importance in our spiritual formation should not be under-estimated.

The third level comes through *financial support.* We cannot be personally involved in every cause, but there are several which we may feel called to support. This too becomes part of a commitment to the world. For funds so given provide the means for people and materials to be used in ministry to others. In recent years we have seen that our money really does make a difference in the lives of others, sometimes even determining whether or not they survive. We must never think of money as impersonal, for it is the expression of the fruit of our livelihood.

To be sure, God will work differently with each of us regarding percentages of involvement. For example, I know some Christians who believe the whole tithe should be given to the local church, while others believe it is all right to divide the tithe. Some Christians believe that personal involvement means they do not have to give as deeply financially, while others pour themselves and their substances into their selected causes. The test is not how you do it, but *that* you do it.

Does it really make a difference? Well, for over twenty years I've been employed in several types of nonprofit organizations. I can testify that the personal involvement and financial contributions of people make all the difference. We sometimes get the impression that churches and large Christian organizations can keep rolling along whether or not we support them. But that is simply not true! Almost every Christian organization and community agency I know of lives on the edge of cutback or extinction. The continued commitment of Christians to the world is the single greatest human factor in determining to what extent our world is reached in the years ahead.

Involvement in these three levels means making a definite commitment to ministry in the world. And such a commitment is indispensable in a healthy spirituality. The final words of Jesus were not to retreat, but to move forward. To be sure, all the personal equipping and maturing possible is necessary, and personal cultivation of the spiritual life is never something to apologize for. But it is all to a purpose—that God can work through us to touch this world until Christ comes again to claim it for Himself. I can't think of a better reason for living.

GETTING OUTSIDE YOURSELF

Look not only to your own interests, but also to the interests of others.   Philippians 2:4

PRACTICE SILENCE

Ask the Lord to reveal areas where you need to extend yourself.

PRACTICE REFLECTION

Examine your expression of Christianity in relation to these missional levels: local church, a hands-on cause, and financial stewardship. Balance positive and negative insights.

PRACTICE RESOLUTION

Complete the following sentence as you believe God would direct: "By the grace of God, I resolve to go into the world _____

_____

_____ ."

PRACTICE PRAYER

Offer yourself as a ministering channel as God directs.

PRACTICE READING

Psalm 72 and Acts 2:40-47

NINE

STREAMS IN THE DESERT

Spiritual dryness is undoubtedly the number one spiritual problem that I discover in myself and in others. It can breed more fear and uncertainty in the Christian experience than anything else I know of. Unfortunately, however, it is not something we talk about a lot. Not much has been written on the subject.[1] Consequently, we are left pretty much in the dark to cope with it when it happens to us.

I had not been a pastor very long before I saw how devastating spiritual dryness can be. One Sunday after our evening worship service, my lay leader asked if he could see me in my study. I could tell by the look on his face that something was wrong. Once inside the office, he wasted little time getting to the point. "My prayer life has been virtually meaningless for nearly eighteen months. I am spiritually dry and depleted. Can you help me?"

I was surprised by his words, for it was the first time I had heard another Christian speak so frankly about his spiritual dryness. But his words have been echoed hundreds of times by others who are experiencing similar things in their lives. I've come to the conclusion that spiritual dryness is one of the best-kept secrets in Christianity. And like wanderers in the desert, we keep going, hoping that somewhere we will find some water.

Spiritual dryness can be met and dealt with as we keep some things clearly in mind. The first is to recognize that spiritual dryness is normal. Every Christian experiences it sooner or later. The problem is that it doesn't feel normal. It hurts. It depresses. It depletes. And since others who may be experiencing it do not show it on the outside, you can believe that you're the only one going through it. In fact, Satan will try to get you to believe that if he possibly can.

There are two primary fronts on which Satan attacks you in this matter of dryness. First, he tries to convince you that you are alone. Have you ever worshiped in a church while going through dryness? If so, you probably noticed your heightened sensitivity to the outward spiritual life of others. You may have even asked yourself, "How can these people be so happy?" Their apparent life only made your lifelessness stand out all the more. You could not see that some of them were as dry as you were, and erroneously drew the conclusion that you were the only one in this soul-wrenching experience.

If Satan cannot get us on that point, he will try to convince us that no other Christian in the history of the faith has ever had our problem or felt as dry as we do. But again, it's a lie. And here is one place where a knowledge of devotional classics can really help, for through them you come to see that the saints of the ages frequently faced spiritual dryness. George Fox endured it for three and one-half years! John Wesley had to battle it even after his Aldersgate experience. St. John of the Cross knew it so well that he wrote extensively about it in *The Dark Night of the Soul*. These insights give us great encouragement, as we realize that even the spiritual giants had prolonged periods when they felt spiritually depleted. So when we go through such times, we can *know* that we are not alone, and not the first to feel this way.

WHY THE STREAM RUNS DRY

But knowledge alone will not deliver us from spiritual dryness, for we need to know the cause. Spiritual dryness is usually a symptom of something else going on in our lives.

† There are people who believe that sin is the chief cause of spiritual dryness. They support this view with the verse, "If I had cherished sin in my heart, the Lord would not have listened" (Psalm 66:18), and imply that sin is the sole or major reason why we become spiritually dry. Their solution is quick and simple: confess, repent, and be healed.

I believe a response to this is needed. First of all, sin *is* a significant cause of spiritual dryness. The Word of God tells us that iniquity will become a wall which separates us from God (Isaiah 59:2). When I am experiencing spiritual dryness, the first question I ask is, "Lord, is there a sin in my life which is choking spiritual vitality?" If something is revealed, I confess it. What I'm saying is that I take sin seriously and begin by asking God to reveal it if it's there.

But the problem in making sin the exclusive cause of spiritual dryness is that it causes us us to miss other factors that can produce it. By limiting dryness to sin, we can create unreal guilt and frustration in people. So, it is necessary to remember that spiritual dryness comes from other sources too.

Therefore, when I'm spiritually dry, I ask God to reveal any sins in my life which might be causing the problem. And there are times when I am convicted. I may be made aware of a sin I've been trying to hide or forget about. Or it may be something which I was not consciously aware of. If that is the case, then I repent and find forgiveness. But if the Spirit does not convict me, then I move on to consider other causes for my dryness. There are a number of others to choose from.

† A second cause is what I call affective breakdown—we simply do not feel alive to God. But this does not automatically mean that we are not alive to Him. We do not always feel loving toward spouse and children, but that does not mean we have actually stopped loving them. We don't always feel like going to work, but that doesn't mean we should quit our jobs.

We experience affective breakdowns in other areas of life

and usually keep right on going. We've come to accept it and do not let it derail us. It's unfortunate that we take a different approach in the spiritual life. Something we accept and treat as normal in other areas, we allow to defeat us in our spirituality. We must recognize the fact that there will be times when our spiritual senses will be dull. Our moods will be down. Our feelings will be dormant. We cannot live on the mountaintop all the time. But when this happens, we can now use what we know in the other areas: the feelings will return and the wells of emotion will flow again.

  † A third cause of dryness is physiological. We are whole people with bodies, minds, and spirits, but these cannot be separated into neat, unrelated categories. In everyday living we function as unitary beings. A breakdown in one area will inevitably cause suffering in our spirits.

  A friend of mine noticed that he would have "down days" spiritually for no discernible reason. He could not point to the weather or to any problem he was facing. It just happened. A Christian counselor told him to chart these swings on a calendar for six months. At the end of that time, he noticed an amazing thing. About every sixteen to eighteen days, he would experience a mild case of spiritual dryness. When he reported this to his counselor, he discovered a possible link between his spirituality and his hormones, and was referred to a medical doctor.

  We cannot experience change in one area without it having some effect in our spiritual condition. We cannot remain spiritually alive if we do not take care of our physical needs, including proper diet, enough sleep and exercise, and stress management.

  Many of our seminarians struggle with this very thing. They come to Asbury spiritually alive, but it is not long before they notice a change for the worse. As I get to know them, I find that in addition to carrying a full load, they are married, have children, and work every evening to make ends meet. Some arrive back in Wilmore in the wee hours of the morning, sleep a few hours, and begin the whole process over again. And in the midst of this crushing schedule, they wonder why they are spiritually dry!

In a society built on superhuman expectations for work and pace of life, we must make allowance for spiritual dryness that is connected to physiological causes. Some of us will not begin to see improvements in our spiritual lives until we make some adjustments in our physical lives. This may mean making some hard decisions relative to our priorities and the schedules we keep. Few of us are able to burn the candle at both ends and remain alive to God.

† A fourth cause of spiritual dryness is underfeeding. Simply put, we are too haphazard and shallow in our relationship with God. I find that this is the main cause of spiritual dryness in my life. I become spiritually dry if I am not intentional enough about my formation, or I let days go by with no devotional acts or with only a tip of my hat to God.

Here again, I learn from a parallel in life. Suppose I only ate a couple of meals a week. It wouldn't be long before I was very hungry and probably sick. Suppose I only spent a day or two each month with my family. It wouldn't be long before they seemed like strangers. The same thing happens in spiritual formation. We become dry because we're starving our souls. God begins to feel like a stranger because we are not spending enough time with Him.

Not long ago, literature about parenting emphasized quality time. The theory had it that the amount of time was not as important as the substance of the time. To be sure, there is partial truth in this notion. But interestingly, writers are now referring to "the myth of quality time."[2] Children need our time in *quantity* as well as quality. It takes time to develop quality relationships.

The same is true of our relationship with God. Quality

must always be the goal, but it cannot happen apart from a commitment to quantity. Each of us faces the need to look at the shape of our lives to see where we can spend meaningful periods of time cultivating a deepening relationship with God. I don't know of anyone in the history of spirituality who lived a life of spiritual depth who was not also committed to spending significant periods of time for the development of that depth.

I am convinced, however, that there is no right amount of time for everyone. The saints reveal an amazing variety in the amount of time they spent in prayer and devotion. Their example is a reminder to me that the same thing will happen today. The retired person's need and opportunities will be different from the homemaker with two children under the age of five. The single person will be able to plan differently than the father who has children in the junior and senior high years. The quantity and quality of devotional life must always be responsive to our stage of life. But at all ages and stages, we will be seeking to find appropriate amounts of time for our formation.

† A fifth cause of spiritual dryness is in trying to imitate the patterns of others. This is a tendency we all face, but it is especially acute in our younger days when we're trying to find ourselves in the faith. We can so easily want to be like our spiritual heroes. We can become overly impressed by things we read and hear.

In one of the courses I teach, I have my students interview a person concerning his or her spiritual formation. I do this for two reasons. First, they can pick up helpful ideas from others that will make a positive contribution to their spiritual formation. But secondly, in almost every case, the students come to see that the spiritual formation of another is a personalized thing. And that's the point. We cannot maintain spiritual vitality if we are trying to model our experience after someone else's.

I honestly believe that God allows us to become spiritually dry whenever our journey is deliberately becoming too much like someone else's. For at that point, we begin to die, we begin to exchange our individuality for an image. And God will not allow us to become a carbon copy of anyone else, no matter how impressive the spirituality of the other is. Some of us will not regain spiritual vitality until we find a style and structure of devotion that reflects our own uniqueness.

† A sixth cause of spiritual dryness is change, which can be environmental, developmental, or spiritual. When we experience significant change, we also notice a change in our spiritual life. If we do not recognize the importance of change, our spirituality will suffer.

I noticed this in our children when we moved from one city to another. As we came to the end of our time in the one place, their questions and prayers began to change. On the one hand, there were doubts and uncertainties which had to be taken into account. On the other hand, there was a sense of excitement as they contemplated the unknown. Our family devotionals had to take these fluctuating emotions into account or there would have been a sense of unreality about our times of worship.

Years ago I heard Bruce Larson tell of a period when his family was facing a major decision. As parents are inclined to do, he and his wife were trying to deal with this matter themselves and shield the children. One night as they were talking, one of their children came into the room. It was one of those times when they had to share what they were talking about with the child. To their amazement, the little fellow thought for a while and in his response cleared up one of the things Bruce and his wife were struggling with. Bruce said that he and his wife learned through that event the importance of bringing children into real-life issues.

Just recently, our family has had to deal with the changes of death, disease, moving, changing schools, making new friends, and helping our children understand the feelings of friends whose parents are going through divorce. All of these changes need to be brought into spiritual formation. There will be times in our lives, sometimes prolonged, when the primary agenda will be the environmental changes which we all face.

Developmental changes must be taken into account as well—those natural, inevitable, biological changes we all face. We could think of it chronologically, in terms of moving from infancy to old age, with all the stages in between. We could think of it relationally—singleness to marriage, unemployment to employment, parenting to empty nest. Such changes can also occur in reverse as we experience divorce, unemployment, the coming of an unexpected baby, etc. These human development events cannot be ignored in our devotional life without our becoming dry.

I was counseling a person who had this very problem. The more we talked, the more I sensed that she was practicing a hothouse devotional life. It had all the right ingredients and looked nice and tidy. But it was largely sterile and unrelated to the dynamics she was facing. As we explored further, we found that her sense of dryness was connected to her omission of real-life issues from her formation agenda. Her devotional life reminded me of tending a very small corner of a garden, while weeds were consuming the rest of it.

Spiritual changes must also be taken into account. As you move along in your faith development, you should be progressing from spiritual milk to spiritual meat (Hebrews 5:11-14). However, like the Hebrews, some people become spiritually dry because they do not get a personal grasp of the basics of the faith before they try to move on to deeper things. In the ministry of spiritual formation, we dare not assume that people have a grasp of the fundamentals. Many do not. And to assume that they do will be to program dryness sooner or later. Taking people too far too fast will only confuse and frustrate them.

On the other hand, some people get dry because they think spiritual milk will continue to satisfy them. They assume that the devotional systems of their early days will suffice all the way to the end. I have to counsel many of my students in this regard. Some of them become dry because they try to force an approach to the spiritual life to work when they have grown beyond it. They need to move from the shallow to the deep. As spiritual life develops, we need approaches and resources that challenge us to grow just as much as the earlier approaches did when we were spiritual infants.

Are you experiencing changes in your life? Make them an integral part of your spiritual formation. Relate Scripture to them. Pray about them. Find secondary material that addresses change. Talk with Christian friends about them. Write the changes in your journal, if you keep one. Bring the concerns with you when you participate in the public worship of God. Get those changes inside the circle of your spiritual life so that the grace of God can deal with them.

† A seventh cause of spiritual dryness may surprise you. In some cases dryness is God's method of getting us to move on to something new or different. For example, if every time I open the Bible, I find great meaning in the Gospel of John, I may never go on to discover the other sixty-five books. No matter how meaningful one part of Scripture may be, the time will inevitably come when the Spirit will prompt me to read elsewhere. And there will also be those times when God leads me out of Scripture in order to find inspiration in the many devotional classics (historic and contemporary) that abound in the Christian tradition. There will even be those times when the focus will not be on reading, but on other means of allowing God to speak, such as music or art.

The same is true of prayer. If every time I pray I am focusing on confession, there will come a time when the Spirit will challenge me to have a more balanced prayer life by including praise, intercession, petition, etc. In addition to different aspects of prayer, the Lord may lead to new and different forms of it—the use of written prayers, silent prayer, prayer partners, etc. The point is that God will not allow us to get our spiritual formation out of balance without attempting to bring us into greater variety and wholeness. These times of spiritual dryness are meant for our development. They should motivate us to try new things and discover new dimensions of the spiritual life.

I had a friend whose elaborate Scripture memory system consumed most of his devotional periods. However, as time wore on, Scripture memory began to lose some of its meaning. Instead of finding it a joy, he found it a chore. It became sterile and mechanical. Since he had put so much energy into it, his first assumption was that there must be something wrong with his spiritual life. But on further reflection and prayer, he came to see that he had focused on Scripture memory at the expense of other things. God was simply trying to broaden him and balance him. When he realized this, the joy of his spiritual life returned. He continued to memorize Scripture, but he also brought some new and exciting features into his spiritual formation.

We all have to struggle with the problem of spiritual inertia. The Israelites grumbled time and again as they wandered in the wilderness, even to the point of wanting to go back to Egypt. The early Christians found it hard to leave the security of Jerusalem for the uncertainty of the pagan world. It took persecution to force them out into the very places God intended them to go all along. We should not be surprised to find ourselves becoming too comfortable with certain styles and practices in the spiritual life. But when we do, we can count on being challenged by the Spirit, sooner or later, to move on. If we resist, we will find ourselves becoming spiritually dry.

† An eighth cause of spiritual dryness revolves around intake and outflow, or what we might call devotional application. A few years ago, I was going through a period of dryness. When I prayed about the cause, I received an answer that was strange at first. The Lord said, "You're dry because your devo-

tional life does not have a back door." A back door? What did that mean? It didn't take me long to realize that while I was being faithful in having devotional times, I was not being faithful in living out the implications of such times. In other words, I was pretty good at going into devotions, but not so good at coming out of them. Intake was adequate, but outflow wasn't.

This is a spiritualized form of conspicuous consumption. It is an approach to the spiritual life which emphasizes accumulation rather than application. In my life it meant that I could have a marvelous devotional time on "patience," but shortly after, I would find myself yelling at the kids. The fruits of my spiritual life were lacking. My head and heart were becoming full of true and powerful information, but they were not passing those insights on to my volition, so that I would begin to act on them.

The old phrase, "Use it or lose it," fits right in here. The spiritual life cannot be hoarded. It evaporates unless it is applied. Remember the Israelites and the manna? The manna could not be stored up. It had to be gathered and eaten on the day it appeared. So too, our spiritual life is for now. The lessons we learn in times of study and prayer are meant to produce corresponding changes in our lives.

As I read Scripture and other devotional literature, I keep a marking pen at hand. I prayerfully search for a word, a phrase, a sentence, or a paragraph that becomes God's Word for me that day. I underline it and spend time reflecting on it. Then during the day, I try to recall it as often as I can and find ways to apply it. At the end of the day, I look back to see how I have done. In this way, I am trying to close the gap between intake and outflow. It has become a method of getting devotional insights off the page and into my life.

† A ninth cause of spiritual dryness is compartmentalization. That's a big word which means keeping our devotional life fenced off from the rest of life. It's related to intake and outflow, but for purposes of study we can think of it

separately. The root problem is that we have come to think of spiritual formation more as having a "devotional time" rather than living a "devotional life." We have so defined our spirituality that we see it as occurring only in designated devotional times.

Here is where a knowledge of the devotional classics can really help us. The saints of the ages knew that true spirituality can never be divorced from the totality of life. Specific acts of devotion are intended to connect with the rest of life. And conversely, any event of the day can be an occasion for encounter with God. Because Jesus is Lord, every moment can be a God-moment. As we read the lives of the saints, we find them discovering God throughout the day, and seeking to increase their perceptiveness to the point of continual devotion—their understanding of "praying without ceasing."

It is this development of continuous devotion which actually makes specific acts of devotion meaningful. We will quickly lose the joy of our faith if we do not find it having any impact on our living. We know that Jesus did not just come into the world to help us believe better, but to help us be better and *live* better. The Christian faith is behavioral, not just cognitive. Spiritual dryness is inevitable when we try to keep our faith in boxes, reserved for special days, events, and seasons.

I've spent quite a lot of time on the causes of spiritual dryness, to show that many things can cause us to become spiritually dry. I've tried to select a variety of reasons, so you can see that it can happen to us on a number of different fronts. While sin must always be taken seriously as a possible cause, it must not be viewed as the sole cause.

REFRESHING MEMORIES

When we are spiritually dry, it is helpful to draw on the resources of *memory*. One of the beauties of the spiritual life is that God does not erase our memories; rather, He heals them. If God erased our memories, too many good and positive experiences would be lost in the process. In times of spiritual dryness, we can feed on memories of past moments when God was near and our faith was alive.

After more than twenty years, I still have some precious memories of several Communion services where the presence of God was significantly at work in my life. Many other high moments as well are stored away in my memory bank. In times of dryness I can make use of those memories to remind me of the reality of my faith and the reality of God. As I've used the resources of memory, I have noticed how important the idea of remembering is in the Bible. Forgetfulness is dangerous in the spiritual life. Memory is a means of restoration, strengthening, and healing.

Dr. Norman Vincent Peale tells of a man who came to him years ago suffering from acute depression. He had come to believe that life was not really worth living. Carefully Dr. Peale began to ask the man to recall precious moments from his past life—beautiful moments when life was good and God was real. One by one, the man pulled these events from his memory bank, moving from years past right up into the present. Each of the memories was like an object laid on the table. By the end of the session, the table was full of real events, people, and situations—each of which served as evidence that life was worth living.

You have that same collection in your mind. That's one of the reasons God has given you memories. In times of dryness, take a cup of coffee or iced tea, go to a quiet place, and let your memories come pouring out. As the old hymn says,

"Count your many blessings, name them one by one,
And it will surprise you what the Lord has done!"

You may want to make lists of your precious memories in a journal, so that you can return to them again and again. You may think, "But if I do that, there will be some painful, unpleasant things which will also come out." That's true, but just let them come, yet filtering out as many of these as you can. As much as possible, concentrate on the good experiences of your life. As you grow in your spiritual life, you will be able to receive the bad memories as well as the good. But if this is new to you, I suggest focusing on the recollection of God's faithfulness, love, and caring in your life.

At the same time, remember that Jesus is victor over the bad and painful moments of your life. These may haunt you, but they cannot hurt you. Christ has died once and for all to forgive you of all the dark moments in your past. I realize that this may not be easy for you to accept. In fact, it may take some counseling before the most painful memories can be healed. But for now, remember that there is nothing which can come from your past which is greater than Christ's power to overcome it. In fact, the good news is that He has already dealt decisively with it on the Cross!

As we grow in our faith, we discover that even the painful past can be used to achieve positive results in the present. In other words, I can learn and grow by even reflecting on my hurts and failures. While this is not pleasant, it can be productive. Who can minister most effectively to alcoholics? Right! Former alcoholics. Who can best help those who are going to have open-heart surgery? Right again! People who have had open-heart surgery. No one wishes for alcoholism or heart disease; but later on, even these painful things can be transformed into useful memories.

Jeannie and I have a friend who has gone through the pain of a relationship with an alcoholic, which included pregnancy out of wedlock. She chose to marry the man, but had to divorce him after a few months. She then went back home to try to pick up the pieces of her life, while at the same time having to rear her child alone. I can tell you for sure that she never intended for her life to take the turns it did, and it has taken years to cope with the scars which it produced. But at the same time, she understands young women who are going through the same thing, in ways most of us never could. God is using her to touch other lives.

Do you have negative, painful memories in your life? You may not have the spiritual strength to bring them to the surface right now. Begin by focusing on the positive aspects of your spiritual life. But be assured there will come a time when you can and should receive the negative memories as well. Through them you will discover new dimensions of God's grace, and maybe even powerful avenues of ministry.

THE RIVERS STILL FLOW

You can be confident that spiritual dryness will not last forever. It never has and it never will. It is *always* temporary. The goodness and warmth of the spiritual life will return. So don't give up. Stay at it. In times of dryness we are tempted to quit. But that's the wrong thing to do. If the renewal of our spiritual life is to take place, we must continue practicing spiritual disciplines.

It is true that you may need to simplify your devotional life. I occasionally counsel people to do some careful cutting back in times of dryness. Why? Because the problem of spiritual dryness is often related to trying to do too many things. This destroys desire. So, I counsel people, "Cut back and pay attention to your heart. When you've cut back far enough, there will be a renewed sense of desire. And that's what you've been looking for in the first place. The recognition of need can become a new foundation on which to build new desires and practices. Don't be afraid to relax and step back a little. For a while, trust more than try."

While cutting back, focus on the enjoyable things in your spiritual life. If you're dry, you may be asking, "What things?" Let me give you a clue. If you had thirty minutes or an hour to spend with God, how would you most like to spend it? Reading? Praying? Listening to music? Writing poetry? Walking? Working in the garden? Playing your favorite sport? Photography? You name it. Then do it to the glory of God. This does not mean that hobbies are equal in value with spiritual disciplines. But it does mean that God may choose to renew you through such a means. The principle is to seek for an end to dryness in those things which have often been sources of joy in your life.

I was talking about this in one of my classes. After the class was over, a student stayed behind to talk. She said, "Before I go I want to be sure I understand what you were saying. And to find out, I want to ask you if it is all right for me to play my guitar during my devotions." I confess I was surprised by her question, but I could tell she was serious. I asked her to explain further.

She told me how each morning during good weather, she would get up early, go outside, and sit on a bench. There she would play her guitar. Some mornings she would compose on the spot. Other mornings, she would play some song that had been written by her or someone else. "Then," she said, "I'd look at my watch and think, 'Well, it's time to quit now and go inside and have devotions.' " She concluded our conversation by saying, "If I heard you right today, you were telling me I've already been having my devotions while I'm playing my guitar."

Exactly! It's so simple, but we miss it over and over. Somewhere we have had the idea that enjoyable things cannot be part of a devotional life. We've excluded talents and hobbies, and for many of us, these are the very things which allow us to express our faith in God. Some of us need desperately to bring these things back inside the circle of spiritual formation. They can be the agents of restoring our confidence and leading us out of times of spiritual dryness. In fact, if we paid more attention to them, we might not feel spiritually dry as often as we do!

"I'm spiritually dry. Can you help me?" I have heard

those words so often that I could not leave this chapter out. Spiritual formation does not ignore dry times. It does not write people off because they have them. It accepts the valleys and the wilderness experiences and seeks to help people interpret them, and to eventually move out of them. Denial only pushes us deeper into the mire of despair. Acknowledgment is the first step toward cure. I cannot tell you how long your dryness will last. But I do know one thing: *it will not last forever*. The rivers of living water will flow again!

MOVING BEYOND DESPAIR

My soul faints with longing for Your salvation, but I have put my hope in Your Word.   Psalm 119:81

PRACTICE SILENCE

Recall a time in childhood when someone came to you in the dark to bring help or comfort, and remember how good it felt to have someone near. Can you recall occasions when God has come like this to you?

PRACTICE REFLECTION

Review the causes of spiritual dryness in this chapter. Does one stand out as being more true for you? Take time to probe it more deeply. Write yourself a "spiritual prescription" to deal directly with it.

PRACTICE RESOLUTION

Determine to remain as obedient and attentive as you can, when you are spiritually dry.

PRACTICE PRAYER

If you're spiritually dry right now, ask a Christian friend to pray for you. If you know someone who is dry, intercede for them. Consider putting feet to your prayer through some word or act of love.

PRACTICE READING

Psalm 13 and 2 Corinthians 1:8-11

TEN

THE EDGE OF ADVENTURE

Sometimes I wonder what it would have been like to have been one of Jesus' original apostles. There are indications that most of the men had had previous contact with Jesus. This contact, though limited, was seemingly enough to convince them of Christ's integrity. And I believe it served as the basis for their ability to receive His invitation to discipleship at a later time.

The invitation was disarmingly simple, "Come, follow Me, and I will make you fishers of men" (Mark 1:17). And equally disarming, to those of us who read the story, is their quick response. By whatever means, each of the Twelve came to the conclusion that Jesus was offering them something they dared not refuse. His invitation had a ring of adventure to it. It offered promise, even if it lacked a clear indication of where it would take them. They knew they were on the edge of adventure, and they wanted to be part of what Jesus was calling them to.

I hope this is how you are feeling—that the invitation to live the spiritual life is an offer you dare not refuse. I hope that you too will sense that you are on the edge of adventure with Christ.

None of us has any more idea of the implications of our discipleship than did those Twelve who first followed the Lord. For us, as for them, the invitation is challenging but not specific. It contains an element of risk and uncertainty. It is the kind of invitation that can be realized only in the fulfilling of it. And if history is any teacher, we see that the invitation will not be experienced uniformly—it is as individual as we are.

In several translations, the word *become* is part of the invitation. The *New King James Version* puts it this way: "Come after Me, and I will make you *become* fishers of men." I believe this is a good translation, because it puts dynamism into the invitation. We find it harder to think of our discipleship as something with a termination point or graduation date. It reveals discipleship as a life that is continually developing and expanding and in which the sense of adventure should never disappear.

While we never graduate or retire from Christ's school of spiritual formation, the sense of adventure is not constant. It waxes and wanes. At times it is so strong that we are almost overwhelmed by it. And at other times, we can hardly tell it is there, and we feel spiritually dry.

In my spiritual formation, I have discovered something that helps to keep adventure in my faith. While it is not automatic or foolproof, it is very valuable to me, as I seek to maintain a sense of development and dynamism which I believe discipleship is meant to have.

It has been beneficial for me to pray this prayer frequently in relation to my spiritual development, "Lord, what would You have me to be doing at this time in my life to grow in Your grace?" I have discovered that as I pray this, I receive fresh insight into the substance and direction of my spirituality. Time and time again, in God's answers to this prayer, He has given me an ongoing sense of adventure in my spiritual life.

† The prayer begins with "Lord." This reminds me that God must always be the reference point in my spiritual development. In a day when multiple ideas and resources abound, it might be easy to think that spirituality could develop along the lines of the latest book, record, or tape. But if I let this happen, I would fall prey to the "cult of the contemporary."

There are many ways to interpret the temptation of Jesus

in the wilderness. But certainly one thing we notice in it is Satan's attempt to make Jesus respond to an outside voice rather than to His own inner dialog with the Father. In each attack, Jesus remained constant through His reliance on the Word of God. He never shifted from absolute attentiveness to the inner directive of Scripture and Spirit.

Across the years, I have seen people get into trouble because they wrongly assumed their growth was completely determined by outside influences and suggestions. This has sometimes resulted in frustration and a sense of aimlessness. They thought they should be reading or doing what others were engaging in. They paid more attention to the suggestions of the group leader or to the current bestseller than they did to the voice of God.

I am not suggesting that we should never walk along paths indicated to us by others. There are certainly times when God guides through the directions of fellow believers. But the outside suggestion should find connection with the deeper, interior voice of the Spirit. For after all, our growth and maturation are a matter of God's guidance. It is to Him that we look for our development. So, the prayer begins with "Lord."

This process of prayerful reflection usually takes some time; and for me, it usually occurs in solitude and quietness. Although the prayer itself is brief, the process may be extended. Making God the point of reference in spiritual growth does not mean that the answers will come quickly. But it does mean that we have committed ourselves to a kind of progress in which our steps are ordered by Him.

When I talk with groups about waiting for God, someone inevitably asks, "What do you do while you're waiting for the next step in your journey?" I answer by saying, "I do what is appealing." This is another way of saying that I turn to those things which I enjoy most. I go back to those books in the Bible which have fed me most in the course of my journey. I pick up a book which I have been wanting to read, but have not been able to find time for up to now. When I do this, I sometimes find that this becomes the means of new direction. But even when it does not, it is an enjoyable and valuable interlude until the more specific direction comes along.

This raises the question of *how* God reveals His will to us. I've yet to find any list of surefire steps for determining if something is from God. Every attempted list has to be matched to the issues at hand. I do believe, however, that we have been created in the image of God, and that we are enabled to know and to do God's will. Such knowing comes from a conscientious use of spiritual disciplines, from involvement in the church, from spiritual direction and counsel, and from deep inner convictions that sometimes defy description. Our knowledge of God's will is not perfect, and we at times misread things. That's why we need to use more than one method in searching for God's will. We need to submit our thoughts to the advice and critique of others. And we need to live humbly, always ready to admit if we make mistakes.

† The next phrase in the prayer says, "What would You have me to be doing . . . ?" Obviously this reinforces the idea that God is the director, but it also introduces two new ideas to the scheme. It introduces "me" into the picture and, by doing so, personalizes the plan of spiritual formation.

I'm sure you've seen that I am for personalization in spiritual formation and development. I believe that one of our most critical mistakes is to exchange our individuality for some image of what the spiritual life is supposed to be. We live in an age which tries to make us believe that our worth and person-hood is to be found in the image we project through the products we buy and the clothes we wear. We hear about the importance of "making a statement" with our clothes or cars, as if these were the only ways of telling the world who we are.

But if we play by such rules in our spiritual development,

we will sell our uniqueness for a neutralized version of the spiritual life. In the early days of our spiritual journey, we may have needed the security and direction of uniformity. But to continue this approach will severely limit what God desires to make of us. As we grow in the life of faith, we should be discovering the grace of God flowing through those parts of our personalities which most uniquely express us.

In the television game show, *To Tell the Truth*, three people would each claim to be the same person. After an examination of each one, the final question was, "Will the real _____ please stand up?" I believe that is a good question for spiritual formation. As you develop in deeper ways, your real personhood should come more and more to the surface, and you should feel less need to live behind a mask or promote some image. The grace of God is liberating you to be the unique, unrepeatable person you were intended to be from the moment of your conception. Now that's adventure!

I trust you know that I am not advocating that you become selfish or self-centered in your spiritual development, or obnoxious in your uniqueness. Spirituality does not mean brashly forging private trails. Remember, your uniqueness is inextricably tied to Jesus. Your individuality is always emerging in relation to an increasing Christlikeness. And in Christ, you are free to be yourself! With God as the continual reference point for your development, you do not have to fear that personalization will lead you off into tangents and extremes.

This sets you free to use the years of your life discovering who you really are in Christ, and who God meant for you to be when He made you. You are not to become a carbon copy of anyone else. So, when you pray the word "me," you can remember that spiritual development takes place in the context of your individuality.

When I was a child, I used to wonder how the florist got so many different colors of carnations. And then one day, a florist friend took me into the workroom and showed me. He took white carnations and placed them in the color of dye he wanted them to be. Gradually, the flowers soaked up the coloring through their stems until they absorbed the intended color.

When you hear, "God has a wonderful plan for your life," you could mistake it to mean that it's a one-size-fits-all plan—suitable for all good Christians. Actually, the key phrase is "your life." God has a color of living all picked out for you. The secret is in allowing yourself to become saturated with it; in allowing the grace of God to increasingly move into your being, enlivening your personhood in ways that could never happen if you held on to a generalized image. Mother Teresa said it succinctly, "Our holiness depends on God and ourselves."[1]

This means that we are active cooperators in the formation process. And that's why the phrase "to be doing" comes at this point in the prayer. I do not mean to imply that spiritual development is a matter of works. For whether in our conversion or our growth, salvation is by faith through grace—not of works lest anyone should boast. We must not repeat the Galatian error of beginning in the Spirit and trying to end up through human effort (3:3). So, erase all notions of works' righteousness from your mind.

But don't erase the fact that God has called you into a holy partnership as far as your spiritual development is concerned. You are not merely a passive recipient of what God has for you. The invitation to the first disciples contains the word *follow*, and subsequent calls for some kind of human response and action. The Twelve did not make themselves disciples, but they did cooperate with Christ as He made them into disciples. So must we.

The phrase "to be doing" therefore speaks of an active formation. It speaks of human responsiveness to divine grace. It means that we are asking, seeking, and knocking as Christ Himself told us to do. In practical terms, it means that when the alarm clock goes off in the morning, we hit the floor and find our way to the place of prayer and devotion. It means that throughout the day we consciously seek for ways to be attuned to the Spirit and to live as those who are committed to Christ. And it means that we end our day in examination complete with appropriate decisions that will lead to more effective discipleship in the future.

It is this cycle of grace and responsiveness that establishes the rhythm of our spiritual formation. It is the spirit of the boy Samuel who said to God, "Speak, for Your servant is listening" (1 Samuel 3:10). It reminds us that the agenda for our formation always rests with God, but that the establishment of that agenda is conditioned by our willingness for God to have His way in our lives.

Numerous times in this book we have discussed various ways "to be doing" the spiritual life. This phrase encompasses many things. Whether through the use of the means of grace, through community, or through service in the world, we are responding to the grace of God. And that dimension must be present if our faith is to remain an adventure.

One of the implications of this is that we may find ourselves emphasizing different things at different times. For example, as I write these words, I am approaching the Bible more systematically, in a slow, verse-by-verse study of a particular book. And at this time, my prayer life has taken on a more structured form using the resources of the Book of Common Prayer. Also, the Lord is working in my life to bring a greater sensitivity to the needs of the world. These are things which I believe God would have me "to be doing" in order to respond to His grace. And if the future is like the past, there will be changes along the way, as other things rise to the surface of priority.

† The next phrase is "at this time in my life." Through these words, I try to capture the developmental nature of spiritual formation. The spiritual life is more correctly described

as a stream than it is as a set of orders. It is something we flow in, more than something we accomplish. And it changes as we change. It addresses us throughout our lifetime in ways that are appropriate to where we are.

When I think back to the early days of my Christianity, I see the need to know the territory. Then I had to spend my time just finding out which books were in the Old Testament and which were in the New. I had to look up all the verses relative to the plan of salvation. I went through Campus Crusade's "Ten Basic Steps Toward Christian Maturity" as a means of familiarizing myself with the fundamental content and shape of the Christian experience. I read the Bible through from Genesis to Revelation. Future spiritual formation was shaped by those early days of foundation-laying.

But nearly twenty-five years later, my formation agenda is vastly different. Life is not the same at forty as it was at fifteen. The questions and problems and pressures have changed. Being married is different from being single. Being a father is different from being a husband without children. And parenting adolescents calls forth new things from me that parenting young children did not. Such changes have to be taken into account if my spiritual life is to develop realistically and meaningfully.

At times I see people trying to use an agenda which does not express where they are now. They're trying to make a fill-in-the-blank approach suffice in a multiple-choice world. The spiritual formation challenge is to match the place where we are in life with the grace of God appropriate for that time in life. This may mean repeating things done in the past, or it may mean adopting new methods and using new resources.

When Moses met God on Mt. Sinai and asked Him His name, God replied that His name was "I Am." At least one of the things He was telling Moses was that He is a present-tense God—a God of the "now." That is the only kind of God who will suffice, for that's where all of us live. We inhabit the past by memory and the future by hope, but we live in the present. By naming Himself "I Am," God was assuring us that He is in the present, to meet with us in the experiences of our lives.

A while back, when my personal devotions were in a stagnant period, I prayed, "Lord, what would You have me to be doing at this time in my life to grow in Your grace?" The answer emerged over a period of time in this form, "Steve, your son, John, will soon be a teenager. You don't know very much about adolescent boys. You've forgotten most of your adolescence, and John is facing a world that is vastly different than when you were a teenager. You need to find out what it means to be the father of a teenage boy in today's world." That was the agenda, clear as a bell.

I mention it because it doesn't sound like typical fare for a devotional time. But for the next several months I used my quiet time to read books on adolescence and to search the Scripture for related insights. I also used the time to pray about John and my relation to him in a new way. The "at this time in my life" phrase brought me to a very necessary step in my spiritual development.

I pray this question in relation to myself, my marriage, my job, my friends and neighbors, my church involvement. And in all these areas, God supplies answers which are sometimes surprising, but always right and deeply meaningful. The phrase, "at this time in my life," keeps the adventure in my faith, because I know that it is God's intention for my formation to be up-to-date with the experiences of my life.

This kind of approach to spiritual formation will keep us from wishing we could go back to some past time of life. Oh, sure, there are times when I wish I could go back to some event or period and savor again the goodness of it. I think of this especially in relation to my children. But in my best moments, what I praise God for is the fact that He is leading me forward into events and experiences that are equally meaningful. The "I

Am" God gives precious memories, powerful promises, and present blessings.

I'm especially thankful for a number of elderly people I've known, who never grew old in spirit, people for whom life was full and exciting right up to the time of death. They have shown me that if I will set my sails to move in the wind of the Spirit at the various times in my life, then even the years of old age can be times of love, joy, discovery, and usefulness. The phrase, "at this time in my life," includes every conceivable time.

† The final phrase, "to grow in Your grace," defines all the others. Cultivation of the spiritual life is for one purpose only— to grow in the grace of God through Christ. Everything else must become a means to this ultimate end. The grace of God is big enough and powerful enough to produce growth throughout a lifetime. This does not mean that each day will be a winner, or that every experience will yield discernible growth. But it does mean that as we step back and look at the long haul, we will see progress.

I do not apologize for using the word "grow" as a real test of my spiritual formation. If what I am doing is not producing growth, then I begin to look for something else. It doesn't matter if a program has been commended by a hundred spiritual experts. If it is not working for me, I keep searching. Jesus *grew* in wisdom, stature, and in favor with God and other people, and this is what God intends for me and for you. If what you are doing is not producing overall growth, drop it and find something else. God may use it in your life sometime later. This is true for me in using formal, written prayers as part of my spiritual development. The first time I tried the Book of Common Prayer, it seemed as dry as dust. But about eight or nine years ago, it came back into my life with meaning, and now I am using it with profit. Just because we lay something down does not mean God will never ask us to pick it up.

I have started more things in my spiritual life than I've

finished. I do not attribute this to a lack of initiative or follow-through, but rather to a quest for growth. I stick tenaciously to anything which facilitates growth, but I turn loose of anything which has lost its ability to produce growth in the grace of God.

A few years ago I completed about half of a devotional work by E. Stanley Jones. After about six months in it, I put it down and moved on to something else. Three months ago, I returned to the book because some of the unexplored portions addressed needs in my life that were on the front burner. The joy is that both in the laying down and in the picking up there is growth, and that is what I'm after.

"Lord, what would You have me to be doing at this time in my life to grow in Your grace?" For me, this has been the question which has kept the adventure in Christianity. It is a question which mixes grace and responsiveness, liberty and accountability, formality and informality, change and constancy. It is a question which personalizes the whole experience into something that etches my soul just as uniquely as God has etched my fingerprints. Yet, it is a question which leads me into a wider fellowship of other believers who are on similar journeys. It takes me into the church from which I draw an overall sense of the kind of journey I'm called to be on. It brings to life for me the confirmation and conviction of the Spirit which are both so necessary to spiritual formation.

Many pages ago, I stated my conviction that this is the kind of Christianity God intends for us all to have, but it is not the kind everyone experiences. So many things can keep it from happening. Jesus has come to be our Saviour, our Lord, and our Friend. Friendship with Jesus brings an exciting sense of adventure to life. The One through whom all things were made is the One who comes to make us into people we could never become without Him.

If we could be together right now, I would want you to know how much I hope something in this book has helped you to see and experience Christianity in this way. I would want you to be praying for me as I continue to flow in the stream of spiritual formation. And I would want to have the opportunity to pray the same for you. If you can, please accept the following written words as my prayer for you:

> Gracious God, for a while now the readers
> and I have been together, sharing ideas.
> I pray that You will enable them
> to find friendship with Jesus
> as the supreme experience of life.
> I pray that the coming days will be times
> of remarkable growth in that kind of faith.
> And I pray that they will keep the spirit
> of adventure all the days of their lives.
> We believe we have been created
> to know You and to enjoy You forever.
> Give us the kind of faith
> that will make this possible for ourselves,
> and for others as we live and witness for You.
> I ask this in Jesus' name, Amen.

YOU ARE IMPORTANT!

Look at the birds of the air, they do not sow or reap or store away in barns, and yet your Heavenly Father feeds them. Are you not much more valuable than they?   Matthew 6:26

PRACTICE SILENCE

Remember how good it feels to know you are loved by God.

PRACTICE REFLLECTION

For the next week, use the prayer described in this chapter as the basis for your reflection. Give attention to each phrase and record any insights which come in the process.

PRACTICE RESOLUTION

Review your list of insights. Put them in priority order and begin to deal with items as God leads in the coming days.

PRACTICE PRAYER

Schedule a half day in retreat. Prayerfully reflect over the whole book. Ask God to highlight and underscore the "pearls of great price" which you have uncovered along the way.

PRACTICE READING

Psalm 8 and Luke 15

FOR FURTHER READING

The following materials are suggested to help you increase your understanding of Spiritual Formation, and more importantly, to help you grow in your faith. Readings are categorized under basic headings having to do with our formation. Most of the books are in print at the time of this compilation. The few which are not can be obtained from most college and seminary libraries in your area. In addition to these resources, please use the footnotes as further means of exploring the various topics developed in this book.

General Readings
1. Leslie Weatherhead, *The Transforming Friendship*
2. Steve Harper, *Devotional Life in the Wesleyan Tradition*
3. Maxie Dunnam, *Alive in Christ*
4. E. Stanley Jones, *The Way*
5. Henri Nouwen, *Making All Things New*
6. Evelyn Underhill, *The Spiritual Life*
7. Alan Jones & Rachel Hosmer, *Living in the Spirit*
8. Iris Cully, *Education for Spiritual Growth*
9. Benedict Groeschel, *Spiritual Passages*

Scripture
1. Robert Mulholland, *Shaped by the Word*
2. David Thompson, *Bible Study That Works*

3. Susan Muto, *A Practical Guide to Spiritual Reading*
4. Thomas Merton, *Opening the Bible*
5. H.A. Nielsen, *The Bible As if for the First Time*
6. Robert Traina, *Methodical Bible Study*

Prayer

1. Harry E. Fosdick, *The Meaning of Prayer*
2. Dick Eastman, *The Hour That Changes the World*
3. Kenneth Leech, *True Prayer*
4. Anthony Bloom, *Beginning to Pray*
5. Maxie Dunnam, *The Workbook of Living Prayer*
6. O. Hallesby, *Prayer*

The Lord's Supper

1. William Willimon, *Sunday Dinner*
2. William Barclay, *The Lord's Supper*
3. Martin Marty, *The Lord's Supper*

Fasting

1. Richard Foster, *Celebration of Discipline* (helpful chapter)
2. Tilden Edwards, *Living Simply Through the Day* (helpful chapter)

Direction/Accountability

1. David Watson, *Accountable Discipleship*
2. Tilden Edwards, *Spiritual Friend*
3. Kenneth Leech, *Soul Friend*
4. Robert Coleman, *The Master Plan of Evangelism*

Personality and Spiritual Development

1. David Keirsey, *Please Understand Me*
2. Harold Grant, *From Image to Likeness*
3. Christopher Bryant, *The River Within*

4. Chester Michael, *Prayer and Temperament*

The Holy Spirit
1. Billy Graham, *The Holy Spirit*
2. Kenneth Kinghorn, *The Gifts of the Spirit*
3. Myron Augsburger, *Quench Not the Spirit*

Discipline and Disciplines
1. Richard Foster, *Celebration of Discipline*
2. Gordon MacDonald, *Ordering Your Private World*
3. Albert E. Day, *Discipline and Discovery*
4. James Earl Massey, *Spiritual Disciplines*
5. Maxie Dunnam, *The Workbook of Spiritual Disciplines*

History of Christian Spirituality
1. Urban Holmes, *A History of Christian Spirituality*
2. Alan Jones & Rachel Hosmer, *Living in the Spirit* (helpful chapter)

Devotional Classics (Introduction to)
1. Tilden Edwards, *The Living Testament: The Essential Writings Since the New Testament*
2. Thomas Kepler, *An Anthology of Devotional Literature*
3. *The Upper Room Devotional Classics*
4. Paulist Press Series, *The Classics of Western Spirituality*

Social Spirituality
1. John Carmody, *Holistic Spirituality*
2. John Carmody, *Maturing a Christian Conscience*
3. William Stringfellow, *The Politics of Spirituality*
4. Dietrich Bonhoeffer, *Life Together*
5. Thomas Kelly, *A Testament of Devotion* (helpful chapter)
6. Henri Nouwen, *Gracias!*

7. Henri Nouwen, *Compassion*

Ministry and Spiritual Formation
1. Edward Bratcher, *The Walk-on-Water Syndrome*
2. Henri Nouwen, *The Living Reminder*
3. Louis McBirney, *Every Pastor Needs a Pastor*
4. Henri Nouwen, *Creative Ministry*
5. Oswald Sanders, *Spiritual Leadership*

Devotional Guides and Prayer Books
1. Rueben Job, *The Upper Room Guide to Prayer for Ministers and Other Servants*
2. Bob Benson, *Disciplines for the Inner Life*
3. John Baille, *A Diary of Private Prayer*
4. Charles Swindoll, *Growing Strong in the Seasons of Life*
5. John Doberstein, *The Minister's Prayer Book*
6. *The Book of Common Prayer*

NOTES

Chapter One

1. Richard Foster, *Money, Sex, and Power* (San Francisco: Harper & Row, 1985).

2. Exodus 19:6; Leviticus 11:44; 19:2; 20:7; 20:26; Ephesians 1:4; and 1 Peter 1:16.

3. Henri Nouwen, *Making All Things New* (San Francisco: Harper & Row, 1981) pp. 36-37.

Chapter Two

1. E. Stanley Jones, *The Divine Yes* (Nashville: Abingdon Press, 1975).

2. Maxie Dunnam, *Barefoot Days of the Soul* (Nashville: The Upper Room, 1975), p. 75.

3. I've found the following resources to be especially helpful in seeing the significance of personality in the spiritual life: David Keirsey & Marilyn Bates, *Please Understand Me*; W. Harold Grant, et. al., *From Image to Likeness*; Benedict Groeschel, *Spiritual Passages*; Christopher Bryant, *The River Within*; and Chester Michael and

Marie Norrisey, *Prayer and Temperament*.

4. The most comprehensive instrument for discovering your personality type is the *Myers-Briggs Personality Type Inventory*. It is available through persons authorized to administer it. Most psychologists and pastoral counselors are familiar with it. A less detailed and more readily available instrument is the *Keirsey Temperament Sorter*, on pages 5-13 of *Please Understand Me*.

5. A helpful inventory based on spiritual gifts is Dr. Kenneth Kinghorn's *Discovering Your Spiritual Gifts*. Also helpful is his book *The Gifts of the Spirit* and Dr. Peter Wagner's *Spiritual Gifts Can Help Your Church Grow*.

6. The gifts of the Spirit are found in Romans 12:6-8; 1 Corinthians 12:28-31; and Ephesians 4:11. Interpreters differ on the exact number of gifts. The number is not as important as the principle of exhaustiveness being discussed in the chapter.

7. I especially recommend Richard Foster's *Celebration of Discipline*, James Earl Massey's *Spiritual Disciplines*, Albert Day's *Discipline and Discovery*, and James Fenhagen's *More Than Wanderers*.

8. Richard Foster, *Celebration of Discipline* (San Francisco: Harper & Row, 1978).

Chapter Three

1. Foster, *Celebration of Discipline*, (San Francisco: Harper & Row, 1978), pp. 1-9.

2. In reading the lives of the saints, I have not found any who did not exercise discipline in their spiritual lives. Yet there is an amazing variety in the ways they disciplined themselves. My conclusion is that discipline is indispensable, but the specific forms and content of the discipline are left to the individual.

3. Kenneth Leech, *Soul Friend* (San Francisco: Harper & Row, 1977).

4. In addition to Leech's book, the following are helpful in seeing how spiritual direction actually takes place: Tilden Edwards, *Spiritual Friend;* Francis Vanderwall, *Spiritual Direction;* Barry Woodbridge, *A Guidebook for Spiritual Friends;* and Kevin Culligan, *Spiritual Direction.*

5. My favorite book on journaling is Morton Kelsey's *Adventure Inward.* George Simmons' *Keeping Your Personal Journal* is also helpful.

6. We are fortunate in having some excellent series devoted to the spiritual classics. Especially noteworthy are, *The Classics of Western Spirituality* and *The Classics of American Spirituality* both by Paulist Press. Multnomah Press has published the *Classics of Faith and Devotion.* The Upper Room has published a helpful series of booklets on the classics entitled *The Upper Room Devotional Classics.* And finally, there are two exceptional anthologies which contain readings from the second century to the present: Thomas Kepler's *An Anthology of Devotional Literature* and Tilden Edwards' *The Living Testament: The Essential Writings after the New Testament.*

7. Walter Trobisch, *Spiritual Dryness*, (Downers Grove, Illinois: InterVarsity Press, 1970), pp. 9-10.

8. Thomas Kelly, *A Testament of Devotion* (San Francisco: Harper & Row, 1941), p. 109.

Chapter Four

1. Henri Nouwen, interview in *Epiphany Magazine*, Winter 1981, p. 61.

2. Gordon MacDonald, *Ordering Your Private World*, (Chicago:

Moody Press, 1985), pp. 64-85.

3. Brother Lawrence, *The Practice of the Presence of God*, paraphrased by Donald Demaray, (Grand Rapids: Baker Book House, 1975), pp. 20-21.

4. Kelly, *A Testament of Devotion*, (San Francisco: Harper & Row, 1941), p. 35.

5. I especially like Dr. William Barclay's commentary on this passage in his *Daily Study Bible: The Letters to the Galatians and Ephesians*, (Philadelphia: Westminster Press, 1958), pp. 215-219.

6. Leighton Ford, *Sandy: A Heart for God* (Downers Grove, Illinois: InterVarsity Press, 1985).

7. E. Stanley Jones, *Growing Spiritually* (Nashville: Abingdon Press, 1953), p. 69.

8. Although the idea of the healing of the memories has been misunderstood and misused by some, I still believe it is an authentic and important ministry for Christians. For more on the subject, I recommend David Seamands' *Healing of Memories* (Wheaton: Victor Books, 1985).

9. Robert Boyd Munger, *My Heart, Christ's Home* (Downers Grove, Illinois: InterVarsity Press, 1957).

10. Dr. William Willimon shared this idea in the 1985 Ryan Lectures at Asbury Theological Seminary. It is expanded in his book, *What's Right with the Church* (San Francisco: Harper & Row, 1985).

11. Leslie Weatherhead, *The Transforming Friendship* (Nashville: Abingdon-Festival, 1977), p. 56.

12. Charles Sheldon, *In His Steps* (Old Tappan, New Jersey: Revell Spire Books, 1963).

Chapter Five

1. E. Stanley Jones, *The Unshakable Kingdom and the Unchanging Person* (Nashville: Abingdon Press, 1972), p. 15.

2. Richard Foster, *Study Guide for the Celebration of Discipline* (San Francisco: Harper & Row, 1983), p. 28.

3. Susan Muto, *Renewed at Each Awakening* (Denville, New Jersey: Dimension Books, 1979), pp. 17-18.

4. Ernest Boyer, *A Way in the World* (San Francisco: Harper & Row, 1984), pp. 76-94.

5. James Fenhagen, *Invitation to Holiness* (San Francisco: Harper & Row, 1985), pp. 67-72.

Chapter Six

1. Nouwen, *Making All Things New*, (San Francisco, Harper & Row, 1981), pp. 21-22, 42.

2. John Doberstein, *Ministers Prayer Book* (Philadelphia: Fortress Press, 1959), p. 287.

3. Susan Muto, *A Practical Guide to Spiritual Reading* (Denville, New Jersey: Dimension Books, 1976), p. 11.

4. M. Robert Mulholland, *Shaped by the Word* (Nashville: The Upper Room, 1985), pp. 53-54.

5. Thomas Merton, *Opening the Bible* (Collegeville, Minnesota: The Liturgical Press, 1970), p. 33.

6. In this regard, I recommend becoming familiar with the Inductive Method of Bible study. It is based upon the English text, with appropriate places to use Hebrew and Greek as you're able. It promotes an in-depth, personal, and application-oriented

approach to studying Scripture. The classic text in this method is Robert Traina's *Methodical Bible Study*. Beginners may wish to begin learning this method by using David Thompson's *Bible Study That Works* or William Lincoln's *Personal Bible Study*.

7. Unfortunately, Christian meditation has been polluted by the intrusion of ideas from Eastern religions and even the cults. For that reason, some have avoided it. However, meditation is a positive action, clearly affirmed in Scripture. When used rightly, it greatly facilitates our formation. The following books will guide you to a healthy understanding and practice of meditation: Richard Foster's *Celebration of Discipline*, Thomas Langford's *Christian Wholeness*, and Harvey Seifert's *Explorations in Meditation and Contemplation*.

8. Thomas Jackson, ed. *The Works of John Wesley*, vol. 11, (Grand Rapids, Baker Book House, 1979), pp. 203-237.

Chapter Seven

1. Nouwen, *Making All Things New*, (San Francisco, Harper & Row, 1981), p. 87.

2. *Ibid.*, p. 83.

3. Dietrich Bonhoeffer, *Life Together* (San Francisco: Harper & Row, 1954), p. 25.

4. Miriam Murphy, *Prayer in Action* (Nashville: Abingdon Press, 1979), pp. 77-78.

5. Kelly, *A Testament of Devotion*, (San Francisco, Harper & Row, 1941), p. 85.

6. *Ibid.*, p. 87.

7. Bonhoeffer, *Life Together*, p. 76.

8. Kendall McCabe, "Spirituality and the Sacraments," *Doxology* magazine, vol. II, 1985, p. 18.

9. Donald Saliers, *Worship and Spirituality* (Philadelphia: Westminster, 1984), chapter one.

10. Nouwen, *Making All Things New*, p. 80.

11. Useful resources to facilitate family devotions are Rosalind Rinker's *How to Have Family Prayers* and Evelyn Blitchingdon's *The Family Devotions Idea Book*.

12. I'm indebted to Ernest Boyer's *A Way in the World* for the ideas in this list. They are expanded on in this excellent book on family spirituality.

13. Bob Benson, *Disciplines for the Inner Life* (Waco: Word, 1985), p. 104. Benson's book is an excellent resource for personal devotions. It combines Bible readings, prayer suggestions, and excerpts from hundreds of devotional writings. This particular statement comes from Basil Pennington's *A Place in the Heart*.

14. Don Joy's two excellent books, *Bonding* and *Re-Bonding* (Waco: Word, 1985 and 1986 respectively) provide valuable information on the limits of male-female relations. These limits must also apply in relationships dealing with the spiritual life.

15. Numerous resources are available today regarding the starting and sustaining of groups. Across the years, I've found the following to be especially helpful: Elton Trueblood's *The Company of the Committed*, Harold Freer's *Two or Three Together*, and David Watson's *Accountable Discipleship*.

Chapter Eight

1. C.S. Lewis, *The Weight of Glory* (New York: Macmillan, 1980), p. 19.

2. Thomas Langford, *Prayer and the Common Life* (Nashville, The Upper Room, 1984), p. 28.

3. Benson, *Disciplines for the Inner Life*, p. 279. Taken from Henri Nouwen's *Gracias!*

4. Nouwen, *Making All Things New*, (San Francisco: Harper & Row, 1981), pp. 28-29.

5. "Are You Making What You're Worth?", *U.S. News and World Report*, June 23, 1986, pp. 64-65.

6. Kelly, *A Testament of Devotion*, (San Francisco, Harper & Row, 1941), p. 109.

Chapter Nine

1. The most helpful resource I've found is Walter Trobisch's *Spiritual Dryness*. St. Teresa of Avila's *A Life of Prayer* provides sound counsel on dealing with dryness. Gordon MacDonald's *Restoring Your Spiritual Passion* is one of the best contemporary works on the subject.

2. Prudence Mackintosh, "The Myth of Quality Time," *Focus on the Family*, May 1986, pp. 10-12.

Chapter Ten

1. Benson, *Disciplines for the Inner Life*, p. 126. Taken from Mother Teresa's *A Gift for God*.